CHRISTIAN HEROES: THEN & NOW

SAMUEL ZWEMER

The Burden of Arabia

CHRISTIAN HEROES: THEN & NOW

SAMUEL ZWEMER

The Burden of Arabia

JANET & GEOFF BENGE

YWAM
PUBLISHING
P.O. BOX 55787   SEATTLE, WA 98155

YWAM Publishing is the publishing ministry of Youth With A Mission (YWAM), an international missionary organization of Christians from many denominations dedicated to presenting Jesus Christ to this generation. To this end, YWAM has focused its efforts in three main areas: (1) training and equipping believers for their part in fulfilling the Great Commission (Matthew 28:19), (2) personal evangelism, and (3) mercy ministry (medical and relief work).

For a free catalog of books and materials, call (425) 771-1153 or (800) 922-2143. Visit us online at www.ywampublishing.com.

CHRISTIAN HEROES: THEN & NOW

Adoniram Judson
Amy Carmichael
Betty Greene
Brother Andrew
Cameron Townsend
Clarence Jones
Corrie ten Boom
Count Zinzendorf
C. S. Lewis
C. T. Studd
David Bussau
David Livingstone
Dietrich Bonhoeffer
D. L. Moody
Elisabeth Elliot
Eric Liddell
Florence Young
Francis Asbury
George Müller
Gladys Aylward
Hudson Taylor

Ida Scudder
Isobel Kuhn
Jacob DeShazer
Jim Elliot
John Wesley
John Williams
Jonathan Goforth
Lillian Trasher
Loren Cunningham
Lottie Moon
Mary Slessor
Nate Saint
Paul Brand
Rachel Saint
Rowland Bingham
Samuel Zwemer
Sundar Singh
Wilfred Grenfell
William Booth
William Carey

*Unit study curriculum guides
are available for select biographies.*

*Available at your local Christian
bookstore or from YWAM Publishing
1-800-922-2143 / www.ywampublishing.com*

Arabia

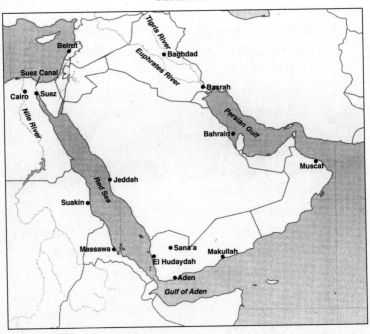

Contents

Chapter 1

Death Stared Him in the Face

Each sailor clung to the side of the large canoe with one arm while trying to bail out water with the other. Everything, including their luggage and the precious cargo of Arabic Bibles, was drenched. The waves were mountainous, each one threatening to capsize the boat. "We are running ashore until the storm is over. We cannot outrun it!" the captain yelled above the wind. Sam breathed a sigh of relief. He did not want to drown, and dry land seemed the safest place to be at that moment.

Sam watched through the sea spray as two sailors wrestled with the oars to bring the canoe around. They then began the difficult task of rowing against the wind and current toward shore. It seemed like forever before he felt the bottom of the boat scrape against the sand. The sailors jumped out—half swimming, half walking—and began dragging the boat to the beach. But this proved too much of a struggle for them, and Sam and his traveling companion Kamil jumped into the sea to help. Working together, they managed to drag the canoe to safety on the beach.

Sam shivered. As he surveyed the desolate beach on which they had landed, he noticed that the captain looked nervous. The captain's eyes kept looking from side to side as if he were expecting to see something. But there seemed to be no civilization for miles in any direction.

Five minutes later, as Sam crouched beside the canoe, sheltering himself from the weather, two Bedouin men carrying long spears and arrows burst onto the beach. Their appearance was so sudden that Sam could scarcely believe it. Sam stood up. He hoped that the captain would step forward and handle the situation, but the captain and the two sailors stood as still as statues, rooted to the sand and paralyzed by fear.

Sam felt his heart thumping as the two Bedouin men walked toward him. The men's menacing spears were pulled back over their shoulders, ready to thrust at Sam at any moment. From the grim look on their faces, the men seemed intent on killing someone. Since Sam was the only non-Arab in the group, they immediately fixed their gaze on him. Sam looked behind him. The storm still raged, and angry waves crashed ashore. There was no escaping back out to sea. Sam and his companions would surely drown if they tried. They had nowhere to run for cover on the beach.

Death stared Sam in the face. This was not a situation he had expected to find himself in when he came to Arabia as a missionary seven months before. It seemed he was about to be killed before he accomplished any of the things he had trained so hard for. He wondered how his family back in the United States would react when they learned that the body of Samuel Zwemer had been found speared to death on a deserted beach on the south coast of the Arabian Peninsula.

Moving

Six-year-old Samuel Zwemer, or Sam, as everyone called him, plunked himself down on a wooden box and surveyed the scene. It was a bright July morning in 1873, moving day for the Zwemer family—the nine younger children and their parents. Sam sighed as he looked at the giant red maple tree in the yard and wondered how he was going to get along in Albany, New York. He had been born in Vriesland, Michigan, but this home in Milwaukee, Wisconsin, was the only one he remembered.

Although the Zwemer family lived in cramped quarters, Sam loved everything about living in Milwaukee. He'd just started school, and since he could already read and write both English and Dutch, he was doing well. He had lots of friends to play with, most of them from church. Sam's father, Adriaan Zwemer, was a pastor in the Dutch Reformed Church, around which much of the family's life revolved. In fact, it was hard for Sam to figure out where church ended and home life began. Members of the congregation visited the house in a continual flow, and Sam's mother, Catherina, welcomed everyone with a bright smile as she served her guests her special Dutch waffles and cups of steaming hot coffee.

Every meal in the Zwemer home began with a prayer and ended with a Bible reading. This morning's passage had been about Moses leading the people of Israel to the Promised Land. "Ja," Sam's father had said in Dutch at the end of the reading (the whole family spoke Dutch at home). "God tells his people to go into all the earth to spread the gospel, and go we shall."

Sam's father went on to recount the story of how he and Sam's mother had come to America as part of the early wave of Dutch immigrants who settled in Michigan, Wisconsin, and Iowa. The Reverend Albertus Van Raalte had led the initial group to leave Holland in 1846 and settle in Michigan. The Dutch immigrants, or Hollanders, had come to the United States partly to escape a bitter clampdown on "unauthorized" churches in Holland and partly because of a severe economic depression that had left young Dutch people with few choices for their future.

Sam knew the story by heart, but it still thrilled him. His father seemed so old now, with his flowing beard and gold-rimmed spectacles. Sam found it hard to imagine his father as an eager young man climbing aboard a ship named the *Leyla* in 1849, bound for the New World. Sam's mother had traveled aboard the same ship, since she was engaged to Sam's father. She was twenty-two years old at the time, four years younger than Adriaan. Although she was born in Holland, her parents were from Germany.

The voyage to the United States lasted thirty-eight days. Sam often asked his father to tell him about the big storm when a giant wave spilled over the stern of the ship, dousing the fire Sam's mother was cooking rice cakes over. "The firebrands almost caused a ship fire," his father would say, "but worse was to come. That wave was the first of many enormous waves. We were soon ordered below deck, and the water leaked in profusely. We 128 Hollanders, under the leadership of Pastor Klyn, spent the night praying. The water below deck rose until it washed over the lower bunks. Everyone climbed onto the top bunks. We thought the ship was sinking, and we were locked below deck. We kept praying. The next day was terrible, but God was with us. Eventually the violent rocking stopped, and then they opened the hold and let us out. The sun was shining, and we breathed the fresh air."

Sam's parents made it safely to New York City but decided not to move all the way to Michigan with the rest of the Dutch immigrants they had traveled with. Instead, they married, settled in Rochester, New York, and quickly produced four babies. Two of the babies survived early childhood and were the "big children"—James and Maud. James, who was now 23 years old, had just graduated from Western Theological Seminary and become a pastor, while Maud was a schoolteacher. Next came the seven "middle" children. Mary, the oldest of these, was seventeen years old, followed by Fred, Catherina, Christina, Adrian, Nellie, and nine-year-old Hettie. Last were the two "little ones"—Sam and his younger brother Peter. The boys were less than a year apart in age, and both had light blue eyes and dark hair. Strangers often mistook them for twins. There had been two other younger children: Anna was born a year before Sam and had died soon after birth, and Hendrik was the youngest child and had died the previous year. Sam remembered how his new brother had been sick from birth and how he had died just before his first birthday. It had been a very sad time for the family, but Sam's parents assured him that one day he would be able to play with Hendrik in heaven.

Now the family, except for the two oldest children, James and Maud, were moving to Albany. Sam had studied the location of the city on the map that hung at the front of his schoolroom. Albany was about level with Milwaukee, but it was far away from any lake or the sea. Sam knew he would miss that. He loved to walk along the shore of Lake Michigan and dream that he was aboard a ship bound for some strange land.

"Sam, help Nellie carry that basket and hand it to Papa." Sam's mother's voice cut through his thoughts. He obediently lifted the nearby basket and carried it to the back of the wagon where his father was standing.

"Dunka," his father said, pulling his pocket watch from his vest pocket. "We need to have this loaded before noon if we're going to make the train."

Sam smiled at the thought of getting aboard a train. He knew a lot about trains; everyone in his class did. The students had traced how the Pacific Railroad now linked America all the way from New York City to San Francisco Bay. Sam was thrilled to think that a boy could get on a train in Milwaukee and just seven or eight days later step off it on the West Coast of the United States. Sam hoped to make that trip one day. For now, taking the train from Milwaukee south to Chicago and then east through Toledo, Cleveland, Buffalo, Syracuse, Utica, and all the way to Albany, seemed like a big adventure.

The Zwemer family managed to pack the wagon on time and were soon seated on the train for the two-day journey. Sam loved every minute of the trip. In Chicago he watched as herds of longhorn cattle stood mooing in the stockyards beside the railroad tracks.

"Those cattle come all the way from Texas," Sam's older sister Mary explained. "Cowboys drove them to the railhead, and then they were loaded into railcars. The railroads have turned towns like Chicago into boomtowns."

As they approached Buffalo, Mary pointed to the land on the far side of Lake Erie. "See that land over there? That's Canada," she said. Sam stared in the direction she pointed, wondering what it would be like living in another country such as Canada.

When the train chugged to a stop in Albany, Sam got the first glimpse of the town that was to be his new home. Albany was bigger than he had imagined, with tall church spires and very old buildings, much older than the buildings in Milwaukee.

"Ja, the Dutch were among the first to settle this area," Mary said. "Albany started off as two trading posts between the Indians and the Dutch colonists way back in the early 1600s. The trading posts were called Fort Nassau and Fort Orange, after the Dutch royal family. New York City was founded by the Dutch too. Did you know that?"

Sam shook his head.

"Well, it was," his sister went on. "It started out as a trading post called New Amsterdam, mainly trading beaver furs from the Indians." Then Mary laughed and patted Sam's dark hair. "That's a lot of information to take in, isn't it? I hope to be a teacher like Maud, and sometimes I practice on you."

Sam smiled. He didn't mind at all. In fact, he loved to learn about the world he lived in.

It did not take long for Sam to settle into the family's new home in Albany. Things soon fell into a routine much the same as that in Milwaukee, with family life revolving around school and the church Adriaan pastored. Sam discovered a love for reading and quickly rose to the top of his class. Books became his friends. Sam would rather curl up in a chair and read a book than do almost anything else. He had two favorite books, one written in Dutch and the other in English. The book in Dutch, *The Family Fairchild*, was about three young English children and their everyday adventures living in a big house in the country. The book in English was *Pilgrim's Progress*, and Sam especially loved its colored illustrations.

Three years in Albany passed quickly, and just after Sam's ninth birthday, it was time for Adriaan Zwemer to leave his church and take up a new pastorate. This time it would be somewhere quite different—Graafschap in Allegan County, Michigan. Unlike Albany, which had a rich, long European history, Graafschap was a tiny frontier town on the eastern shore of Lake Michigan. Many people warned Sam's father about taking his family to such a place, and one of Sam's friends even taught him the rhyme, "Don't go to Michigan, that land of ills. That word means ague, fever, and chills."

When Sam asked his sister Catherina whether this was true, she did not give him a direct answer. Sam wondered what his new home was going to be like. Would Michigan be as wild as everyone said it would be?

Soon Sam was aboard another train with his family as they journeyed west.

When the Zwemers arrived at Graafschap, Sam felt like he had stepped into another world. The village was not at all like Albany. It was made up of frontier houses clustered together in a clearing that had been carved out of the surrounding forest. It had a general store and a little red schoolhouse where

Sam would attend school. As was customary in such communities, the church formed the center of village social and spiritual life. Most people spoke Dutch and wore Dutch clothing and clogs.

The Zwemer family soon adjusted to life in Michigan. Sometimes after school, when they were not reading books, Sam and his younger brother Peter would roam in the woods around the village, pretending they were missionaries going to some dark corner of the world. As they clambered among the trees, they had to step around the burned stumps and trunks of old ones. These trees had been burned in the Great Fire that had swept through the area five years earlier in 1871, just days before a huge fire also swept through the city of Chicago across Lake Michigan. The fire had not only burned the trees but also burned many houses and killed hundreds of people. The area had a lot of low-lying swampland that harbored mosquitoes and disease, but by now much of this swampland was being drained. The reclaimed land was being used to grow a new vegetable that was catching on in the United States—celery.

Sam enjoyed helping his father in his workshop. Adriaan Zwemer loved to make things from wood. Such items as chairs, tables, and bedsteads flowed out of his workshop behind the house. Between his pastoring duties and making furniture, Sam's father found time to make the family a croquet set, complete with mallets and balls. Sam loved watching his father shape the wood on his lathe and then sand it until it was perfectly smooth and beautiful.

During the hot summers, Sam swam in the river and sometimes was invited to go sailing on Lake Michigan. He didn't like group sports, but during winter he enjoyed ice skating on the frozen river.

It wasn't long before Sam's four older sisters all became public school teachers. They banded together to help put Fred through Hope College so that he could become a pastor like Sam's oldest brother, James. James and his wife now had three little girls, Katrina, Maria, and Henrietta, making Sam an uncle three times over.

By the time Sam finished elementary school in 1879, Hope College, the Reformed Church's university in nearby Holland, Michigan, had expanded to include a high school. The new school, Hope Academy, provided a four-year course designed to prepare students to enter university. Sam was enrolled in the first class of twenty students at the new school, half boys and half girls. Attending the new school would involve a four-mile walk to Holland in the morning and back again to Graafschap in the afternoon. Because such a walk would be pleasant in summer but an impossibly difficult trek during the long, snowy winter months, Sam's father decided that his son should board with a Christian family in Holland during the week and return home on weekends. This was a daunting plan for twelve-year-old Sam—being expected to excel at school, away from home. As his older sister Nellie helped him pack his clothes into a well-worn leather bag, Sam wondered how lonely it would be without his close-knit family around him.

Chapter 3

Time to Stand Up and Be Counted

The leaves of the surrounding trees had just begun to turn to shades of bright yellow and red as the Zwemers' wagon rolled along toward Holland, Michigan. Sam sat in the front seat beside his father. He felt very grown up, even more so when his father asked him to recite two of his favorite questions from the Heidelberg Catechism. Sam could recite all 129 questions and answers from the catechism by heart.

Sam began, "Question one: What is thy only comfort in life and death? That I with body and soul, both in life and death, am not my own, but belong unto my faithful Savior, Jesus Christ; who, with his precious blood, hath fully satisfied for all my sins, and delivered me from all the power of the devil; and so preserves me that without the will of my heavenly Father, not a hair can fall from my head; yea, that all things must be subservient to my salvation; and therefore, by his Holy Spirit, he also assures me of eternal life, and makes me sincerely willing and ready henceforth, to live unto him."

Sam paused for a moment as his father patted him on the knee and spoke. "Never forget that, son. God has the power to deliver you from *all* evil. You just have to ask him to do so. Now, go on."

After taking a breath, Sam recited on. "Number twenty-seven: What dost thou mean by the Providence of God? The almighty and everywhere present power of God; whereby, as it were by his hand, He upholds and governs heaven, earth, and all creatures; so that herbs and grass, rain and drought, fruitful and barren years, meat and drink, health and sickness, riches and poverty, yea, and all things come not by chance, but by his Fatherly hand."

"Ja. Ja," Adriaan said. "You know, it is one thing to recite these things, Sam. It is quite another matter to have them stored in your heart, ready for the trials you will face. Everyone faces trials, but it's the Christian man or woman who has prepared for them ahead of time who gets through them. If you are in trouble, if you don't know what to do, remember that God is the beginning and the end of all matters and that everything that happens to you is not by chance but by Providence. You have been given a wonderful opportunity to learn. Seize hold of it and become the best student you can possibly be. These next years will lay the foundation for your future."

Sam knew that his father was right. He hoped to do well enough at school to go on to Hope College in four years and follow the example of his brothers, James and Fred.

Things started off well for Sam at Hope Academy. He was a natural student who already had a firm grasp of Dutch, English, and German, and he took quickly to learning Latin and Greek. He also studied math and science, both of which he excelled in. He was particularly interested in biology and would spend time wandering through the woods surrounding the school, picking berries and flowers to study. Spare time for such activities, though, was limited. During the week schoolwork came first, followed by chores for the Engles, the family with whom he boarded.

On Friday afternoons Sam would pack a few clothes and walk the four miles home to Graafschap for the weekend. He spent Saturday helping his father or studying, and Sunday was taken up with attending Sunday school and church. It was a busy, happy life.

The first year at Hope Academy flew by, and soon it was time for Sam to return home for the summer. Back home in Graafschap, Sam found work with the local blacksmith. The work was hard, mostly carrying coal and stoking the forge (coal hearth), but Sam enjoyed watching the blacksmith form shapes out of the hot, glowing orange metal as he pulled it from the forge.

In the fall, Sam returned to Holland for another year of school, only this time his younger brother Peter went with him and also boarded with the Engles. It felt good to Sam to look out the window during class and every now and then catch a glimpse of his brother.

Another two years at Hope Academy passed. During his second summer in Graafschap, Sam worked as a clerk at the local grocery store. He put aside the money he earned to help pay for his food and board during the following school year.

Sam knew that his first responsibility was to get good grades, but he did take time out to contribute to the school newspaper, the *Excelsior*. He often wrote poems and literary compositions for the publication. One of the pieces he wrote for the paper was a poem titled "True Courage," of which Sam was very proud. The poem grew out of an English assignment to write about a character trait each student admired. Sam thought about the topic for a long time before picking up his pen. He dipped the nib in the inkwell and wrote:

> True bravery never seeks the laurel-crown,
> Her fame extends into a higher sphere,
> Her praise is sounded through eternity!
> He, who, when plodding on life's thorny path
> As oft as care or want his way oppose,
> Doth overcome these obstacles and rise again
> And still march on, is truly brave.

As Sam wrote, he thought about all the older Dutch people he knew who had risked their lives to start a new life and Christian community in America. He wondered whether he would ever be called to show that kind of courage in his own life.

On April 12, 1883, just after his sixteenth birthday, Sam completed high school at Hope Academy. His mother made him a special batch of *speculaas* (Dutch windmill cookies) for the occasion. Sam loved these spicy Dutch cookies molded into unique shapes, and he enjoyed celebrating his success with his family.

That summer Sam again worked as a clerk in the local grocery store, stocking shelves with dried goods and helping customers find what they were looking for. He knew just about everyone who came into the store, and many customers asked about his plans for the future. Sam had no hesitation giving them an answer. He felt that God had called him into full-time Christian work just like his father and older brothers. He assumed that this would be as a Dutch Reformed pastor. The next step toward attaining this goal was to earn a degree in liberal arts at Hope College.

In the fall Sam headed back to Holland, where he enrolled at Hope College. Many things were familiar to him. During his time at Hope Academy, Sam had walked around the grounds of the college many times. Six of the twenty students from his high school class were in his college freshman class. However, instead of boarding with the Engles, Sam joined the other first-year students living in a dormitory. This was not much of a transition for Sam, since it reminded him of living with his big family back in Graafschap.

Each student enrolled at Hope College studied Greek, Latin, German, and French. This posed no problem for Sam, who already spoke German and had studied Greek and Latin for four years in high school. The school also strongly emphasized the sciences, and Sam was required to take chemistry, geology, and botany. Botany was his favorite subject, and he continued to collect plant specimens to study from the woods near his home and around the college.

Mornings at Hope College began at eight o'clock with a chapel service, where the students were reminded of the history of the school. Albertus Van Raalte, who had led the initial group of Hollanders to settle this area of Michigan, had established the college. At the school's founding in 1851, he had given a speech in which he said, "This is my anchor of hope for this people in the future." As a result, Hope College's crest featured a circle with an anchor in the center and the school's motto—*Spera in Deo* (Hope in God)—directly above it.

Faith and hope in God seemed natural to Sam. Like his parents and older brothers and sisters, he had dedicated his life to God when he was so young he could barely even remember it. Yet it was real to him, and during his time at Hope College Sam's faith grew and matured. He loved to listen to the chapel talks and made a point of reading the Bible through once each year. When the pastor of the Reformed Church in Holland called for volunteers to teach

Sunday school at the Pine Creek settlement across the river, Sam volunteered. He enjoyed the three-mile walk each way to Pine Creek from Holland. It gave him time to pray for the young students in his Sunday school class.

During his first summer vacation from Hope College, Sam found work with a threshing gang. He was six feet tall, taller than most of the crew, and was wiry and strong, but it was still the hardest work he had ever done. The gang would go from farm to farm, cutting wheat and feeding it into a threshing machine. Once separated from the stalks, the grain was poured into sacks that were then loaded onto wagons to be taken to market. Although the work was hot, dusty, and backbreaking, the job paid well, and Sam was able save his earnings to pay for his entire tuition the following year. Sam's younger brother Peter joined him on the threshing gang. Because he was to start attending Hope College in the fall, he also needed to earn money to pay his tuition.

The following summer, Sam found a line of work that suited him much better than the threshing gang. He became a book agent, selling books door-to-door. In the course of the job he walked many miles with a satchel of books on his back. Sometimes he would stop beside a stream and read from one of the books he was carrying. He told himself that this would help him to sell the books better. The truth was, he loved to read any book he could get his hands on.

In August 1886, between Sam's junior and senior years, tragedy struck the Zwemer family. After being ill for several years, Sam's mother, Catherina, died at age fifty-nine. On one of Sam's last visits to see his mother, she told him something that had a deep impact on his life. "I'll never forget it, Sam," she said, patting him on the back of his hand. "As I placed you into the cradle for the first time, I prayed that God would make you a missionary, and I've never doubted since then that you would become one."

The funeral for Catherina Zwemer was one of the largest held in Holland, Michigan. All of Sam's family attended, including his brothers Fred, who was now a missionary in the Dakotas, and Adrian, now a businessman in Sioux City. As sad as he was at the death of his mother, Sam felt even sadder for Adrian, who had married two years before. His wife, Jenny, had died soon after giving birth to their son, John. Unable to look after John alone, Adrian had brought his son back to Graafschap for his parents to look after. Now Catherina Zwemer was gone, and John needed someone else to step in and look after him. Maud, who had been teaching school for ten years, offered to live with their father, keep house, help him run the estate, and care for John.

Sam's father composed himself enough to speak at the funeral. "Mother traveled with me, as did Sarah with Abraham, as we journeyed from Europe to America, and then through the length and breadth of this land, from Albany in the East to Milwaukee in the West," he began. "Mother will always remain in my thoughts, and my heart says like David, 'She will not return to me, but I shall go to her.' Four of our children await her in heaven, and doubtless she is with them again. What a joyous reunion it will be when we are all together."

The sun shone brightly as the funeral procession made its way to Pilgrim's Home Cemetery in Graafschap, where Catherina Zwemer was buried.

Adjusting to life without his mother was difficult for nineteen-year-old Sam, especially since his father accepted a call to a new church soon after her death and moved to Middleburg, Iowa. The Zwemer family was now spread throughout the Midwest. Sam's six older sisters had government teaching jobs and gave part of their income to help Sam and Peter through college.

During his final year at Hope College, Sam attended a meeting in the college chapel. The billboard declared that Robert Wilder, a brilliant young student from Princeton University, was going to speak on "A Call to Missions." Sam hoped it would be an interesting night. It turned out to be life changing.

Robert was about Sam's age and spoke with a strong Eastern accent. He began his address by explaining to the audience how he came to be touring many of the colleges in the United States.

"This summer I was at Mount Hermon in Massachusetts, where D. L. Moody organized a one-month summer conference," Robert declared. "While I was there I asked Mr. Moody if I might have an evening to speak on the matter of missions. He agreed, and I rounded up nine other students who could talk with authority on missionary work. I became the tenth person in the presentation, since my parents were missionaries in India and I spent the first fourteen years of my life there.

"The response was remarkable—and unexpected on Mr. Moody's part. Exactly one hundred students signed pledge cards, giving themselves to the preaching of the gospel around the world. Some will go, others will stay and pray and raise money, but everyone will have a vital part in bringing the good news of the gospel to every person on earth in this generation. We are calling ourselves the Student Volunteer Movement for Foreign Missions."

As he listened, Sam felt goose bumps rising on the back of his neck. This was just what he was looking for—a group of young people with a passion for missions. He leaned in closely as Robert continued.

"Being a missionary comes at great personal cost; there is no doubt about that. God asks us to give up the things that are more precious to us in order to obtain the pearl of great price. In the Book of Matthew, chapter 13, verses 45 and 46, it says, 'Again, the kingdom of heaven is like unto a merchant man, seeking goodly pearls: Who, when he had found one pearl of great price, went and sold all that he had, and bought it.'

"God asks us to give up the good for the best. It is not easy. At this moment my father lies at home in his bed, dying, and a part of me wants very much to be with him. When I felt God called me to tour colleges, I resisted because I wanted to spend my father's last days beside him. I put this to him, and he took his time before responding. 'Son, let the dead bury the dead. Go thou and preach the kingdom.' I do not expect to see my father again until I join him in heaven. But what a reunion it will be, knowing that I have followed in his footsteps."

Sam felt tears welling up within him. It had been only seven months since his own mother had died, and he often thought about the way she urged him to live a godly life and give himself completely to God.

Robert Wilder continued. "John Wesley once said, 'Give me a hundred men who fear nothing but God, hate nothing but sin, and are determined to know nothing among men but Jesus Christ and Him crucified, and I will set the world on fire with them.' Who among you will join the Student Volunteer Movement and help us to set the world on fire for Jesus Christ? Come down to the front and show God you are serious about fulfilling the Great Commission. 'Go ye into all the world and preach the gospel, and lo, I am with you, even unto the end of the age.'"

At these words Sam's heart beat so loudly he was sure those around him could hear it. He knew that God was calling him to be a missionary, and it was time to stand up and be counted. He joined several other Hope College students making their way to the front of the college chapel. As he glanced back, Sam saw that his brother Peter was among them.

Sam stood at the front, praying quietly as Robert finished speaking. Then he signed his name on the Student Volunteer Movement card, pledging to give his life to the advancement of the gospel in whatever way he could. It was a pledge he would keep for the rest of his life and a moment he would think back to when he had important decisions to make.

Chapter 4

Three Spokes

Sam returned to his studies with renewed vigor. He now knew for sure that he was called to be a missionary—he just didn't know where. But this did not concern him too much. He knew he had a lot to do before he could go to the mission field. First he had to finish college and then complete three years of seminary training.

Sam did think seriously about what he should do for summer. Working in the grocery store or on a threshing gang or selling books door-to-door would not help equip him to be a missionary, but he soon found something that would. The American Bible Society (ABS) was expanding all over the world, translating, printing, and distributing Bibles. As Sam read thrilling accounts of the Bible being presented for the first time to people who spoke Mandarin, Japanese, Zulu, and Gilbertese, he wanted to be a part of the adventure. The most effective way to do so was to become a colporteur—a representative of the ABS who walked the highways and byways, meeting families in their homes, reading extracts from the Bible to them, and talking to them about their spiritual needs. Because he had only a few months before beginning seminary training, Sam chose to become a local colporteur.

Classes at Hope College ended six weeks before the official graduation ceremony, and in May 1887 Sam set out to equip himself for his summer job. His first task was to buy a horse and cart, which together cost ninety-six dollars. It was a lot of money, but Sam was sure it was a good investment in his future.

The job as a colporteur for the American Bible Society sounded easy enough—meet people who would not normally have access to a Bible, read it to them, and offer to sell it to them for a small sum of money or, if they were destitute, give it to them. The challenge, as Sam soon learned, was that many people said they were too busy to stop and listen as a Bible story was read to them. The colporteur's manual suggested that in such cases the colporteur offer to work alongside and talk to the person about Christianity as they labored together. Sam found this method to be very effective, and he was grateful for all the time he'd spent with his father building things in the workshop. He could pick up a chisel or file to help a wheelwright or use his previous summer job experience working with a threshing gang for a few hours in order to talk to the men during one of their breaks. Sometimes he even sat with the women of the house and shelled beans or wound cotton—anything that would help start a spiritual conversation with people.

Despite its many challenges, Sam loved the work. Some days he would lead the horse and cart for twenty miles, walking along muddy cow tracks. He would often be invited to stay the night with a family, but sometimes he was run off a property and had to pitch a tent by the side of the road.

On June 22, 1887, Sam was back in Holland, Michigan, for his graduation ceremony from Hope College. It was a proud moment, though he had to hold back tears as he thought about how much his mother would have loved to see him graduate. Following graduation it was back to his work, trying to get a Bible into every home in the district.

After three busy months as a colporteur for the ABS, summer was over, and it was time for Sam to make a final decision about where to attend seminary. Sam was not sure where to go. His oldest brother James was now a professor at Western Theological Seminary, the seminary extension of Hope College. Going there seemed sensible, but his brother Fred urged Sam to attend McCormick Seminary in Chicago, which he had attended. Another option was New Brunswick Seminary in New Jersey, from which Sam's father had graduated.

Sam was still not sure which seminary to attend when he headed to a Zwemer family reunion in

Alton, Iowa, close to Middleburg, where his father now pastored a Reformed church. Sam and Peter caught a steamship across Lake Michigan to Milwaukee and then took a five-hundred-mile train ride to Middleburg. When they arrived, Sam was excited to see his father again and to meet the congregation he pastored.

The landscape around Middleburg was very different from Graafschap. Middleburg sat on flat prairie land and was surrounded by cows grazing contentedly, and there was no lake nearby. Still Sam enjoyed himself, especially when the rest of the Zwemer family showed up for the reunion. He enjoyed hearing the stories his brother Fred and his new wife told about their adventures as missionaries to the Dutch settlers and Indians in South Dakota.

During the reunion, attention was also focused on which seminary Sam should attend. After several long conversations with his father and brothers, it was decided that New Brunswick Seminary in New Jersey would be a good choice. The consensus was that attending this seminary would broaden Sam's experience. Sam was thankful for his family's input and happily accepted their decision.

Sam arrived in New Brunswick at three o'clock in the morning in September of 1887. The first thing that struck him about New Brunswick Seminary was the wonderful Gardner A. Sage Library. The library, having been completed less than fifteen years before, was modeled after a fourth-century cathedral. Sam loved the sweeping archways and alcoves of books, each with a beautiful stained-glass window at the end of it. Best of all were the books—all one hundred thousand of them. Most were written in English, Dutch, German, or Latin, and Sam was grateful he could read all four languages.

Student life at seminary quickly settled into a routine. Sam was assigned to room 32 in Hertzog Hall along with several other young men from the Midwest. It was comforting for him that other students also came from small towns.

Sam set right to work on his two priorities, studying and preparing himself for the mission field. From the first day, he committed himself to spending his lunch hour, between twelve and one o'clock, reading his Bible and praying. Soon the idea caught on, and other students joined him. Sam joined the nearby Suydam Street Reformed Church, where he sang in the choir and taught Sunday school. He also immersed himself in the missionary opportunities the seminary provided. In October, just one month after arriving, Sam was a delegate to the Inter-Seminary Missionary Alliance held in Alexandria, Virginia. Attending the gathering and meeting with so many other young people with a call to missionary service inspired him even more.

Sam prayed hard about his next steps and came to the conclusion that it would be useful to understand medicine as well as theology. However, since New Brunswick Seminary did not offer courses in medicine, Sam decided to read through a copy of *Gray's Anatomy* on his own. He took lots of notes as he read, and when he had finished the book, he found another medical textbook to continue his personal study.

On January 24, 1888, Sam preached his first sermon. The act of preaching came naturally to him, since he had heard thousands of sermons by his father and older brothers. After giving the sermon, which was on missionary work, Sam had an inspired idea. He wondered whether the seminary students and faculty would be willing to sponsor their own missionary. By eleven o'clock that night, he had $150 pledged toward the support of a missionary, and by the end of the week, he had raised the astonishing sum of $700. The Reverend Louis Scudder, a doctor from India, was chosen to receive the money.

Besides reading books for his course work, Sam read a wide range of missionary biographies. He was struck by one about George Müller, a German man who had gone to England and cared for thousands of orphan children. When he had finished the biography, Sam wrote, "George Müller's life of trust makes one feel the power of prayer. Why can we not all live in that way?"

Sam determined to do his best to live the kind of life that George Müller had been living. He prayed that God would show him the specific place where he should be a missionary. Slowly Sam felt his heart warm toward the people of Arabia. The life of a young man named Ion Keith-Falconer inspired him in this. Ion was the son of a wealthy Scottish earl and had been a popular figure in the British Isles. In addition to being a scholar in Arabic, he was a world champion cyclist and a devout Christian. Ion and his new bride had moved to Sheikh Othman, near Aden in South Arabia, to help with a Free Church of Scotland medical clinic and to open an orphanage. Less than a year after going to Arabia, Ion had died from malaria. That had been only six months ago. Ion's willingness to leave fame and fortune at home in the British Isles and sacrifice his life to spread the gospel had a profound impact on Sam.

Ion's story underscored just how difficult working in Arabia would be. Not only was the Arabic language difficult to learn, but missionaries had also largely ignored the region. As a result only a few missionary stations were situated around Arabia, and most of those had been established in the previous twenty years. Deadly diseases and the hatred that many Muslims had for Christians combined to make the area a mission field for which few volunteered.

Sam was not the only student at the seminary who felt a call to Arabia. Two other young men, James Cantine and Philip Phelps—both set to graduate a year ahead of Sam—also wanted to go there as missionaries. The three students began meeting together weekly to pray about their joint calling. James Cantine, or Jim, as everyone called him, and Sam soon discovered how different their backgrounds were. Although both came from homes that were steeped in Dutch Reformed traditions, Jim had been raised on a farm in Ulster County, New York. He had graduated from Union College as a civil engineer and after three years of working in the field, resigned to train to become a pastor.

Jim had not felt any kind of call to missionary service until he attended Dr. John Lansing's classes at the seminary. Dr. Lansing was New Brunswick's Hebrew and Arabic professor. His father, Dr. Julian Lansing, was a well-known scholar and missionary in Syria and Egypt. Because John Lansing had been born in Egypt and spent much of his early life in the Middle East, he was able to bring the cultures of the region to life in his classes. His descriptions of the needs in Arabia moved not only Jim but also Sam and Philip.

Soon Sam, Jim, and Philip took up the study of Arabic. Sam found the language easier than did his two companions. He credited this to the fact that he had been exposed to several languages as a young child. Still, Arabic was challenging. Dr. Lansing called it the "language of angels," and the three students joked that that was because no human could master it.

In his second year at New Brunswick, Sam's younger brother Peter began studying at the seminary. The two brothers continued their close relationship, praying and studying together. Sam also took his medical training one step further. He wasn't yet sure where in Arabia God was calling him, but he had a definite sense that wherever it was it would involve medical work. Because of this, Sam arranged to spend his weekends in New York City helping out at the Bleecker Street Mission. This mission welcomed all sorts of people, from young girls trying to make a living on the streets to old immigrant couples who had nowhere to live.

Sam soon struck up a friendship with William Wanless, a dedicated young physician who worked at the mission and had his sights set on missionary work in India. The two men often talked about missions as they filled prescriptions for drugs. William wrote the prescriptions while Sam counted pills into the bottles. The Bleecker Street Mission had a firm tradition of pasting a printed Bible verse on each bottle of medicine it dispensed. In a moment of inattention, Sam upset one very sick patient when he pasted the verse, "Prepare to meet thy God" onto a bottle. From then on Sam read every Bible verse before sticking it onto a medicine bottle.

At the same time, Sam was in demand as a preacher in the Student Volunteer Movement. He gave as much time as he could to the cause. On September 11, 1888, while in the Midwest visiting his family, he spoke at a large Christian rally at Wheaton College in Wheaton, Illinois. At this rally thirteen students signed declaration cards to become foreign missionaries. Nothing pleased Sam more than having played a role in their decision.

In November 1888, Sam, Jim, and Philip confided in John Lansing that they wanted to set up a mission in Arabia. The professor was delighted to hear the news and quickly rallied to help the three students get started on their new venture. The first step was to get the Reformed Church Mission Board to accept them as their missionaries. This was no easy task, but Dr. Lansing was a respected and well-connected man who was sure he could influence his colleagues to accept the challenge of a missionary thrust into Arabia.

By the spring of 1889, Sam had high hopes that the mission board would soon accept him and his two friends as missionaries. Dr. Lansing attended the General Synod meeting that was held in Catskill, New York. The men at the General Synod shook their heads when the idea of a new mission in Arabia was raised. As far as they were concerned, the church's missionary arm was already in serious debt, and many mission fields, especially China, were under-staffed. It did not seem to them like the right time to open up another mission station.

Sam and his two friends were disappointed when Dr. Lansing told them that they would not be accepted as Reformed Church missionaries, but they refused to be defeated. They felt God had called them to be missionaries to Arabia, and set out to find another way to do just that.

Three months later the young men had their own meeting in Catskill with Dr. Lansing. It was a time of soul-searching and commitment. Philip had a serious family situation that he felt stopped him from con-tinuing with plans to go overseas, but he pledged to do all he could to help the mission from within the United States. Sam and Jim were more determined than ever, though Jim reported that he was encoun-tering opposition from his family. His mother was over seventy years old, and his sisters were urging him not to go overseas until she died. Nonetheless, Jim pressed on with his plans, though Sam could tell the lack of family support was making it difficult.

At the meeting with Dr. Lansing, plans were set in motion to form an independent, nondenominational mission to the Arabs. Everyone hoped that such a mission would be taken over by the Reformed Church of America once it was up and running. For now, the three students and their professor were responsible to set it up. They began outlining the new mission's aim, its name, and how it would raise and distribute funds. The title for the mission was the easy part: the Arabian Mission. The aim of the mission was clear to everyone from the start: to reach Muslims in Arabia with the gospel.

The most difficult challenge would be raising the money to get started. Jim was a year ahead of Sam and due to graduate. The group hoped that he could be sent out right away as the Arabian Mission's first missionary, with Sam to follow the next year.

The four men decided to form a syndicate that would ask for donations of between five dollars and two hundred dollars a year. One person or a group of people could give that amount, or even a group of churches could come together to pledge a certain amount. The money would be spent on sending out and providing the salary for a missionary, while everyone else associated with the mission would be a volunteer.

Now all the Arabian Mission lacked was a logo, a motto, and a song, all of which were decided on quickly. The logo became a wheel with three spokes, with each spoke representing the three students who had started the mission: Jim, Sam, and Philip.

The motto came from a prayer Dr. Lansing had often repeated at earlier prayer meetings: the prayer of Abraham. "O that Ishmael might live before thee!" This was selected because according to the biblical record, the people of Arabia were largely descendants of Abraham through his firstborn son Ishmael.

For the song, Dr. Lansing composed a hymn to encompass the new mission's aims and beliefs. When Sam heard him sing it for the first time, it brought tears to his eyes.

There's a land long since neglected,
There is a people still rejected,
But of truth and grace elected,
In His love for them.
Softer than their night winds fleeting,
Richer than their starry tenting,
Stronger than their sands protecting,
Is His love for them.

By the time Sam left the meeting in Catskill, he believed the Arabian Mission would become a reality. The syndicate funding approach, which they named the Wheel Syndicate Plan, soon appeared in many church newsletters and created a lot of interest. Almost immediately Sam set out to raise money and prayer support among the churches in the Midwest. Jim did the same in the East while preparing for his own departure to Beirut, Lebanon, where he planned to spend his first year improving his Arabic language skills.

Wherever Sam traveled, he made friends and found people interested in his new mission endeavor. On the train to Syracuse, New York, he spoke with Bishop Foster of the Methodist Church. The bishop was so impressed by all Sam told him that he asked for a copy of the Wheel Syndicate Plan to publish in the Methodists' *Christian Advocate* magazine.

From September 2 to October 6, 1889, Sam worked tirelessly representing the new mission. He wrote in his diary, "It may be of interest to give the list of churches where offerings were given or syndicates started: Free Grace, Orange City, Newkirk, Sioux Center, Alton, Milwaukee, Alto, Zeeland, Holland, Overisel, Graafschap, and several churches in Grand Rapids." The total amount of money collected was only about three hundred dollars, but most of the churches signed up as part of the syndicate, which meant they committed to giving the same amount each year.

On October 7, Sam took the train to spend a few days with Jim before he sailed for Beirut. When he returned to New Jersey, Sam was delighted to learn that Christians from many denominations had given gifts and bequests to the new mission. The first bequest of five thousand dollars was from a Presbyterian woman, a friend of Dr. Lansing. In all, there was enough money in the bank to pay for Jim's passage and his first year's salary—and the promise of more to come.

New Brunswick Seminary hosted a reception for Jim on October 16, 1889, at which the seminary's students gave him a set of binoculars, declaring that he could use them to "spy out the land" for the Arabian Mission. One student at the reception remarked that the mission was sure to be a success because "this is a strong outfit—Zwemer is sure to get somewhere, and there Cantine will stick."

The following day Sam stood dockside and watched as the *City of Rome* sailed over the horizon with Jim aboard. He prayed that things would go smoothly for Jim and that in just one year, he too would be aboard ship headed to Arabia.

Chapter 5

Arabia at Last

Sam's final year at New Brunswick Seminary was busy. He talked with anyone who was interested in the Arabian Mission and met regularly with Dr. Lansing to pray and plan for the mission's future. Soon letters arrived from Jim, who had made it to Beirut in time for Thanksgiving. Jim was living in Suk-el-Gharb, a village on the spur of the Mount Lebanon range, where a school for boys called the American Boarding School was situated. Living in Suk-el-Gharb served two purposes: Jim was able to teach the boys English, and he could practice his Arabic language skills. In his letters to Sam, Jim wrote about two young men with fascinating stories.

The first man, Jedaan, was a Bedouin from the Anazy tribe who had been sent to Suk-el-Gharb in

49

1887 to sell sheep for his family. Soon after arriving in the village, Jedaan noticed a man sitting in a shop reading. Hardly anyone from his tribe could read, and Jedaan became fascinated with the idea. "Can a Bedouin learn to read?" he asked the man.

"Yes," the man replied. "Anyone from anywhere can learn to read. Why do you ask?"

Much to his own surprise, Jedaan announced that he wanted to learn. The man did not laugh, as Jedaan had expected. Instead, he sent him to talk with Ibrahim Ahtiyeh, a Protestant teacher at the British Syrian Schools in Beirut who happened to be spending the summer at his house in Suk-el-Gharb. Ibrahim gave Jedaan an Arabic alphabet card, and Jedaan began to learn the letters. Day after day he studied the alphabet while leading his sheep to pasture on the mountain near the village. He would constantly ask passersby the names and sounds of the Arabic letters and simple words.

By the end of the summer, Jedaan was able to read basic sentences and eager to learn more. Ibrahim found a place for him at the school in Beirut, where Jedaan began attending chapel services and Sunday school. Jedaan felt drawn to Christianity and was baptized on February 21, 1889. His faith was simple and clear, and he seemed anxious to equip himself not only to write letters and keep accounts for his tribe but also to teach the people the Word of God and the teachings of Jesus Christ. Jedaan had transferred to the school in Suk-el-Gharb at the same time Jim Cantine was sailing to the Middle East.

The second young man Jim mentioned in his letters home to Sam was a Syrian named Kamil Abdul Messiah El Aeitany. Kamil arrived at the Suk-el-Gharb school after Jim had arrived and became instant friends with both Jim and Jedaan. He came from a different background from that of Jedaan. Kamil could read and write Arabic, and he had attended a military school where he learned Turkish. Kamil also liked to think about religion, and he soon had many questions about his Muslim faith. He decided to go to the Jesuit college in Beirut and study under the Catholic priests there. The priests gave him an Arabic New Testament to take home and read. When Kamil's father saw the New Testament, he burned it in the kitchen fire.

The next day one of the Jesuit teachers told Kamil to take another New Testament and this time tell his father that he had bought it to write a tract attacking its message. That way his father would surely let him keep it. Jim related in his letter how Kamil had confronted the priest. "'Do you advise me to lie to my own father? Never!" Kamil left the New Testament and walked away. Yet his questions remained, and he could not rest until he had answers. He wondered why he could not find anything in the Koran that showed him how God could be a just God and yet pardon a sinner. He knew he was a sinner and that God was just, but it was impossible for him to think of God having mercy on sinners and still being just.

Eventually Kamil found his way to the home of Dr. Henry Jessup, a veteran American missionary. Dr.

Jessup talked with Kamil for a long time and then offered him the use of his own study whenever he wanted. That way Kamil could quietly study the Bible without angering his father. Dr. Jessup also spent many hours answering Kamil's questions and suggesting books and passages from the Bible that Kamil might like to read and compare with the Koran.

Kamil proved to be an earnest Bible student. After a month of studying every day, he decided to profess Christianity and devote his life to preaching the gospel to Muslims. Since Kamil was fluent in the Turkish language, Dr. Jessup suggested he go to Suk-el-Gharb and teach Turkish in the boys' school. At the same time he would be surrounded by Christian teachers who could help him with his Bible knowledge and understanding of Christianity. Once Kamil arrived at Suk-el-Gharb, Jim offered to teach him English, and the two young men became strong friends.

Sam loved reading Jim's letters, and he sent out prayer letters urging his friends to pray that Kamil and Jedaan would soon become missionaries to their own people.

In the meantime, Jim wrote about a walking trip he had taken with an English evangelist and a Scottish missionary along the Mediterranean coast from Beirut to Sidon, Tyre, and Haifa, and through Palestine to Jerusalem. The whole walk was a distance of about 150 miles one way. Of his trip Jim reported, "It was thought a rather hazardous trip, and we were questioned as to what we would do if we were attacked by bandits. The answer was, 'The Scotsman will fight, the Englishman pray, and the American run for help.'" Sam chuckled when he read this. He could imagine Jim sprinting across the desert looking for aid.

Sam worked hard to get excellent grades in his seminary studies. He also found time for his medical studies and visiting anyone he thought might be interested in praying for or donating to the Arabian Mission.

The class of 1890 graduated from New Brunswick Seminary in May. Sam was ordained as a pastor in the Reformed Church on May 29, a month and a half after celebrating his twenty-third birthday. Following his graduation and ordination, Sam had time for a quick trip home, after which he planned to set out to join Jim in Beirut.

Sam's father and brother Fred had both decided to travel to the Netherlands. Sam's father, who was now sixty-six years old, wanted to visit the land of his birth, and Fred was curious to see Holland for himself. The two men booked berths on the SS *Obdam*, the same ship on which Sam would be traveling. The vessel was bound for Bristol, England, where the three Zwemer men planned to take a train north to Edinburgh, Scotland. Sam wanted to visit Ion Keith-Falconer's mother and meet the board of the Church of Scotland Mission to South Arabia, or Scottish Mission, as most people referred to it, which had sent Ion to Arabia as a missionary.

The night before the departure, Dr. John Lansing preached a rousing farewell sermon based on

1 Samuel 30:24–25. He challenged all of those who stayed behind to become involved in the Arabian Mission in whatever way they could. He used these Bible verses to show that God would reward them for their faithfulness, just as he would reward Sam and Jim for going out as missionaries to Arabia.

On June 28, 1890, Sam, Fred, and their father climbed the gangplank of the *Obdam* and waved to the well-wishers below. Sam was grateful for all the people who had supported him so far. He hoped that he could join Jim in bringing life and hope to thousands of Muslims. He used the voyage across the Atlantic Ocean to study Arabic and enjoy times of prayer with his father and brother.

Before long the SS *Obdam* docked in Bristol and the three Zwemers were soon on the train north to Edinburgh. As the train moved along, Sam peered out the window at the rolling green countryside where sheep and cattle grazed. It was similar to what he had viewed from train windows on his trips around the United States, except for the ruins of ancient castles and forts that dotted the English and Scottish landscape.

The Zwemer men were met at the Edinburgh train station by a member of the Scottish Mission board and taken to Lixmount House, where the countess dowager of Kintore, mother of Ion Keith-Falconer, welcomed them warmly. Sam and his brother and father spent a delightful few days at Lixmount House. The countess was a devout Christian who had given birth to seven children, four of them boys. Two of her sons had died as teenagers, and now Ion was also dead, leaving only her oldest son, Algernon. At the same time that Ion had set out to be a missionary in Arabia, Algernon had been appointed by Queen Victoria as governor of South Australia, where he now lived with his wife and children. As the countess told Sam about her family, she wiped a few tears from her eyes but then brightened up when reminding him that those who have died were already rejoicing in heaven.

Sam also met with the members of the Scottish Mission board, who told him about their plans to dedicate a mission hospital in Ion Keith-Falconer's memory. Sam promised to do what he could to help them.

Their stay in Edinburgh over, the Zwemers boarded a train, this time bound for London, where Sam realized that this would be his last time in an English-speaking city for a long time. He took the opportunity to visit bookstores and buy a few books. His best find was Charles Doughty's *Travels in Arabia Deserta*. The two-volume book had been published the year before. The author, an Englishman, had attached himself to a Bedouin group and written about wandering with them through Transjordan and northern Saudi Arabia, all of which were loosely under the rule of the Ottoman Empire. Sam found Doughty's book to be riveting reading.

After spending time in London, the three Zwemer men boarded a ferryboat for the trip to the Netherlands. Sam knew his father was proud to be returning to his home country with two of his sons, who were both pastors. Adriaan was even more proud that they were both missionaries, one in the Dakotas, the other bound for Arabia. In Holland the men were invited to speak at churches in Rotterdam, Leiden, and Middelburg, where the congregations were interested in Arabian missionary work.

Sam's father loved preaching in his native tongue, but Sam was a little worried about doing so. He spoke Dutch and had prepared and delivered one or two short addresses in the language back in Iowa. But now, in the center of Dutch literature and culture, he felt nervous. During the first meeting he titled his talk *Bakermat van den Islam* (Cradle of Islam), but he mispronounced the words so that their meaning came out, "baker's assistant of Islam." Everyone laughed at his mistake but still listened to what he had to say.

Wherever he went in Holland, Sam made friends easily and gained supporters for the Arabian Mission. While in the Netherlands Sam also got to meet some of his relatives. Although many Boons (his mother's family) and Zwemers had originally planned to go to the United States, his parents were the only ones who actually made the journey. Both sets of his grandparent had died long ago, but Sam was able to meet one aunt, two uncles, and numerous cousins.

From the Netherlands, Fred and Adriaan accompanied Sam on a boat up the Rhine River as far as Mainz, Germany, where Sam said farewell to his father and brother and boarded a train for Trieste, Italy. Sam's father and Fred would return on the boat to Holland on their way back to the United States. Once in Trieste, Sam transferred to a ship that sailed down the beautiful east coast of Italy, around the tip of Greece, and eastward to Beirut, Lebanon.

On August 7, 1890, Samuel Zwemer stepped off the ship in Beirut. Jim was waiting on the dock to greet him. The two men shook hands heartily. Jim looked well but was decidedly thinner and had a deep tan. As the two men made their way through the streets of Beirut, Sam was overwhelmed with how different this city was from anything he'd seen in the United States. Beirut was set on low hills beside the Mediterranean Sea. It was a cluster of various architectural styles that reflected the different powers that had controlled the city over its five-thousand-year history.

The streets of Beirut were narrow and flanked by mud-brick buildings, many sporting high arches and columns. Mosques dotted the city and were immediately identifiable by their tall minarets from which people were called to pray five times a day. The streets were alive with people and animals. Sheep bleated, donkeys brayed, and the people seemed to talk at the top of their voices, creating an unrelenting cacophony. The smell of exotic spices and incense emanated from the bazaars and markets. Sam felt as if he had stepped right into one of the paintings of Bible times he used to see at Sunday school.

Sam's arrival in Beirut was followed by a whirl of activity as he was introduced to the wide range of missionaries Jim had come to know. One of these

missionaries was seventy-two-year-old Dr. Cornelius Van Dyck. Sam took an immediate liking to Dr.
Van Dyck, who never seemed to be in a hurry yet
had achieved a remarkable measure of success. He
had taught Arabic, Hebrew, theology, astronomy,
and mathematics, and was a medical doctor and an
ordained pastor. Cornelius Van Dyck was a well-
respected Arabic scholar. Over a seven-year period
he had translated the entire Bible into Arabic. He had
then traveled to New York to supervise the printing
of the Bible.

Sam asked Dr. Van Dyck if he had any advice on
learning Arabic. The old man shook his head. "To
learn Arabic properly is a seven-day-a-week job. The
only way to do it right is to neglect all English papers
and books and read, talk, and think only in Arabic.
Then you will have made a beginning." Then to Sam
and Jim he added, "You have a difficult road ahead of
you. Do not be discouraged if the number of converts
is small. I have never forgotten what my father said
to me as I was unsuccessfully trying to bring down
a bird from the flocks of crows that flew over the old
Kinderhook farm. 'Keep on shooting, my son. They
will fly into it sometimes.'"

Next, Sam and Jim visited Dr. Henry Jessup, the
man who had helped Kamil study the Bible. Dr. Jessup was delighted to meet Sam and gave him some
advice: "The best time to come here is when your
mind is still young and flexible. I was called to Arabia when I graduated from Union Theological Seminary in 1855, and I have never regretted it. I've lived

long enough to see the Syrian Protestant College flourish and the Syrian Church of Beirut well established. I've been offered other roles. Seven years ago the United States government asked me to be the US minister to Persia, but I turned the invitation down. I am the ambassador for the King of kings, and I want no more than that. Helping young men like Kamil hear the gospel is the greatest privilege a Christian can have."

Sam nodded at Dr. Jessup's words. He was eager to meet Kamil himself, but that would have to wait since Kamil had accompanied Jedaan back to his Bedouin tribe to proclaim the gospel to them.

After adjusting to his new surroundings, Sam watched as Jim spread a map of Arabia on the table between them. The area that stretched from Turkey in the north, along the Mediterranean coast to North Africa, and encompassed the entire Arabian Peninsula was vast. Many different tribes and people groups populated the region. As they pored over the map, Sam and Jim firmly believed that God had a special place for them to plant the Arabian Mission— He had just not revealed it to them yet. The two men prayed each day that God would make it clear where they were to go. In the meantime, Sam joined Jim in Arabic lessons and wandered the streets of Beirut, learning about the local culture and talking to people in Arabic.

A month later Sam and Jim were still praying about the location of their mission when they received a telegram from Dr. Lansing, their former professor at New Brunswick Seminary. Dr. Lansing was in Cairo, Egypt, and he invited Sam and Jim to meet with him. Sam and Jim were eager to go. Not only would the trip provide them the chance to see more of Arabia, but also, now that they had experienced Muslim culture firsthand, they were eager for any more advice Dr. Lansing could offer.

Chapter 6

Across the Red Sea

Sam and Jim took a boat from Beirut to Alexandria, Egypt. The history of Egypt stretched back over five thousand years, and Sam was eager to see the country he had read about in the Bible. As the ship sailed along the curving coastline of the Nile Delta, Alexandria came into view on the horizon. Sam could hardly wait to set foot in this city, which, along with Rome, had once been considered a major seat of Christianity. He knew the Church of Alexandria once had jurisdiction over the entire continent of Africa, but that over the centuries this church had split to form the Coptic Orthodox Church of Alexandria and the Greek Orthodox Church of Alexandria. Alexandria had once also housed the world's greatest library. Sam wished he could have seen it. The accounts he had read of the library described it as magnificent.

After a day spent seeing the sights of Alexandria, Sam and Jim transferred to a smaller steamer for the trip up the Nile River to Cairo. Sam loved to stand on deck as the vessel chugged along the Nile. He watched as it passed small mud-brick villages hugging the riverbanks and farmers working fertile fields. Sam learned that between June and September each year the river flooded in a season the Egyptians called *akhet* (the inundation). It was this annual flooding that made the land along the Nile so fertile for farming.

Cairo emerged straddling the Nile, and soon Sam and Jim were standing in the ancient city. As soon as they stepped ashore, young Egyptian boys immediately swarmed around them, hoping to escort them to see the marketplace and the pyramids for a few coins. Instead, Sam asked one of the boys to guide them to John Lansing's Cairo address.

Dr. Lansing welcomed Sam and Jim into his home. Sam was shocked to see how pale and gaunt his former professor looked. It was as though he had aged a decade in just a few months. Dr. Lansing explained that shortly after Sam left for Arabia his health had taken a sudden turn for the worse. As a result he had decided to come with his wife to Cairo, the city of his youth, to see whether a change of climate and location might help him recover before he returned to his teaching responsibilities at New Brunswick Seminary. He apologized for the fact that his wife was not able to greet them, as she was sick in bed.

As Sam and Jim drank tea, Dr. Lansing plied them with questions about their impressions. Sam confessed that he was having great difficulty making himself understood in Arabic. There were so many subtle variations in the sounds of words, and he was having difficulty telling them apart. Dr. Lansing smiled, though his reply was not particularly encouraging: "I learned the language as a boy, surrounded by those who spoke it, but it was still a challenge. But I would rather traverse Africa from Alexandria to the Cape of Good Hope than undertake mastering Arabic a second time."

Following a meal, the three men got down to the business of discussing where the Arabian Mission should put down roots. They spread a large map of Arabia on the table and began to pray over it. A long process of going through the pros and cons of the many potential sites for mission stations followed. The discussions took days as Dr. Lansing patiently explained many aspects of Arabian culture and customs. He pointed out that most missionaries spent their time working among the Coptic and other Orthodox Christians, many of whom had fallen into superstition and tradition and knew little of the true power of the gospel. The missionaries thought that if they rekindled the faith of these Christians, they in turn would go out and preach to the Arabs. But for the most part this strategy had not worked.

Dr. Lansing also explained why so few missionaries felt comfortable preaching directly to the Arabs. There were three main challenges. First was the

language barrier; it took years to learn basic Arabic
and a lifetime to perfect it. Second, it could be dangerous preaching to the Arabs, many of whom were not
tolerant of foreigners telling them that Christianity
was the only way to know God. And third, if an Arab
did show interest in the gospel and spent time with
a foreign missionary, his life could be in danger. Dr.
Lansing explained that this was because Arab families were large and extended and everyone watched
over what everyone else was doing. In his few weeks
in Arabia, Sam had already noticed this. Arabs did not
have freedom to choose their own paths. If their indi-
vidual decisions reflected poorly on the group, there
were consequences. It was not unusual to hear stories
of Christian converts being killed by family members
who were angered that they had changed religion.

As the three men studied the map and prayed,
many places came to mind. In particular Dr. Lansing favored working alongside the Scottish Mission
at Sheikh Othman, an oasis town eight miles inland
from the Port of Aden. Sam felt goose bumps rising
on his arms at the possibility of working in the place
where Ion Keith-Falconer had given his life spread-
ing the Christian message.

Sam and Jim agreed that they should go to Aden
to meet with the leaders of the Scottish Mission
and see whether there was a place for them there.
Jim decided to go on ahead, taking a large steamer
directly from Suez down the length of the Red Sea to
Aden. Sam wanted a few more language lessons with
Dr. Lansing and chose to stay in Cairo for another

week before taking a slower steamer to Aden, one
that would stop at many small coastal towns along
the way.

On January 8, 1891, Sam left Cairo. He was sad
to leave Dr. Lansing behind. Seeing him again had
been such an encouragement. As Sam left, Dr. Lansing read Psalm 107:23–24 and 30 aloud: "They that
go down to the sea in ships, that do business in great
waters; these see the works of the LORD, and his wonders in the deep. . . . So he bringeth them unto their
desired haven."

"There's a promise for you," Dr. Lansing said
when he had finished reading the whole psalm. "I
may not live to see it fulfilled, but it is a promise
from God. You will find your desired haven in Arabia. No matter what happens, don't be discouraged.
Don't give up." He then took Sam's hands in his and
prayed a blessing over him.

Soon Sam was rolling along across the desert by
train from Cairo to Suez. When he arrived at his destination several hours later, he got his first glimpse of
the Gulf of Suez, the northern reach of the Red Sea.
The sight sent thrills down his spine. Over the years
Sam had read many times how Pharaoh had repeat-
edly refused to free Moses and the Hebrew slaves
and how God had visited ten plagues on the Egyptians. Finally Pharaoh let the slaves go free, and the
people marched to the shore of the Red Sea. But then
Pharaoh changed his mind and sent his army after
the people to return them to servitude. God, though,
parted the waters of the sea to allow the children of

Israel to cross to safety. The Egyptian army drowned as the water of the Red Sea flowed back after Moses and the people had crossed. Sam had marveled at the story and the miracle God had performed, and now here he was, staring out at the Red Sea. It was as if his Bible picture book had come to life before his eyes.

Suez sat at the site of another marvel, a marvel of engineering called the Suez Canal, which allowed ships to pass through the desert from the Mediterranean Sea to the Red Sea. The town of Suez sat adjacent to the southern entrance to the canal.

From the train station, Sam made his way to the waterfront. He purchased a second-class ticket aboard a Turkish tramp steamer bound for Aden at the southern end of the Red Sea. The man in the shipping office shrugged when Sam asked how long the trip would take. "It depends on many things," he told Sam. "Cargo can take a long time or a short time to load, and there may be passengers to drop off or pick up at any number of ports. Thank Allah that it is not time for the pilgrims to embark for Jeddah, or seven or eight hundred more passengers would be joining you. Also, it is not unknown to stop for ship repairs."

When Sam looked at the ship, he understood why it might be required to stop for repairs. The vessel looked run-down, and rust streaked her hull. As he strolled down to board the steamer, Sam realized he had quite an adventure ahead of him. Crates and barrels and boxes of dates and spices were being loaded into the ship's hold. A parade of passengers, including brightly dressed Africans, Arabs, and Indians on their way back to India boarded the ship. Just as Sam boarded, he caught sight of two European men. The older man wore a black suit and wide-brimmed black hat, while the younger man wore white. Sam waved to them, knowing that he would have plenty of time to find out who they were once they set sail.

Soon the steamer cast off from the dock and pulled away from her moorings, beginning the fourteen-hundred-mile journey down the long, narrow Red Sea to Aden. At its widest point, the Red Sea was about 220 miles wide. As Sam stood on deck, the two European men approached him. The older man thrust out his hand to shake Sam's, announcing, "I am the Reverend Thomas Valpy French, and this is my companion, Mr. Alexander Maitland. Glad to make your acquaintance."

Sam's mouth dropped open. Standing in front of him was the former Anglican bishop of Lahore, Pakistan. Sam knew of him by reputation. Mr. French had left England in 1850 for India, where he served as a missionary with the Church Missionary Society. He founded St. John's College at Agra in India before being posted to Lahore, where he was appointed first bishop over a large diocese that included Lahore as well as the Punjab and northwestern India. He had also founded the Lahore Divinity College and supervised the translation of the Bible into the Hindustani and Pashto languages.

As the ship steamed down the Gulf of Suez, the heat became intense. Sam found that sitting on the poop deck was the coolest place on the vessel, as did Mr. French and Mr. Maitland. Sam chatted with Mr. French, who explained that bad health had forced him to return to England in 1887. He was now feeling much better and at age sixty-six was determined to start a mission station in Muscat, Oman. Sam told him about the Arabian Mission and his plans to meet up with Jim Cantine in Aden to find a suitable location to establish it. Thomas listened and encouraged Sam in his missionary endeavor.

Two days after setting out from Suez, the ship dropped anchor off the city of Jeddah. Sam climbed down from the steamer into a small *sambuk* (local sailing boat) to take the mile-and-a-half trip to shore. The coast around Jeddah consisted of barren low hills, but the city itself was beautiful. There were many two-storied houses, and each house was decorated with richly carved latticework. The bazaar was crowded and abuzz with the noise of people bargaining for the best price with stall owners. While in Jeddah, Sam visited the Tomb of Eve near the Mecca Gate.

In the late afternoon Sam caught a sambuk back to the ship, where he found Thomas French resting on the poop deck. The bishop explained to Sam how he had gone ashore with two Arabic Bibles hidden in his coat pockets and had found opportunities to give short addresses sharing the gospel. One mullah, or Muslim cleric, had even asked for a copy of the Bible, and Thomas had handed one over to him. Sam was impressed by the man's courage. The Bible was forbidden in Jeddah, and a person openly possessing one could be attacked and even killed by a mob. But Thomas had taken two with him, and not only that, he had preached openly in the streets. Sam chuckled to himself as he imagined Thomas French preaching. Thomas spoke classical Arabic, not the everyday Arabic the residents of the city spoke, and Sam wondered whether those who heard him had understood anything he said.

From Jeddah, the steamer headed in a southwesterly direction across the Red Sea to Suakin in Sudan. Suakin was an ancient and run-down port. There Sam encountered a Christian man, Dr. Harpur, and several helpers who were involved in relief work caring for about sixty orphans in a large tent. On Sunday, while they were still docked in Suakin, Sam attended the communion service that Thomas French held for the relief workers at the home of the Belgian consul.

From Suakin, the ship steamed south for a day and a half through rough waters along the western shore of the Red Sea. The pitching and rolling of the vessel made Sam seasick. Even after the ship had docked in Massawa and he had gone ashore, Sam could feel the effects. Massawa was now part of the newly established Italian colony of Eritrea, and the Italians were busy consolidating their control over the region by constucting palatial buildings throughout the port. Cafes and trattorias abounded along the seaside and were frequented by Italians and people from all over Europe.

On the outskirts of Massawa was a Swedish mission house, which Sam visited with Thomas. The mission was staffed by two Swedish pastors and two women. Sam was impressed by the way they cared for and fed over eight hundred starving people a day with supplies they received from Sweden and the United States.

From Massawa, the steamer headed back across the Red Sea to the eastern shore and the port of Al Hudaydah, where they anchored two miles off the coast and had to be ferried ashore by sambuk. Al Hudaydah had many active bazaars and was loosely under the control of the Turks.

Later that night Thomas told Sam how he had met a high-ranking Turkish officer in Al Hudaydah who sat and listened as Thomas preached. "He seemed struck more by my message, I trust, than by me. When he retreated, he sent down a handsome and really useful walking stick to me, which I felt bound to recognize by making my way up, as best my wearied feet could, to his fine room at the top of the steps. The officer accepted a copy of the entire Bible and kissed my hands with an affectionate transport of gratitude," Thomas recounted. He then added, "Now and again one gets little proofs of God's blessing and helpful countenance in work that cannot help being often discouraging."

Sam nodded. By now he knew firsthand how challenging and discouraging sharing the gospel with Muslim Arabs could be. Yet his enthusiasm to see the Arabian Mission established was not diminished.

From Al Hudaydah the steamer headed south through the straits of Bab-el-Mandeb at the entrance to the Red Sea, passing the island of Perim to port and into the Gulf of Aden. Fifteen days after setting out from Suez, the Turkish tramp steamer reached Aden.

Chapter 7

Aden

The first thing that struck Sam as he disembarked ship in Aden was the large number of British soldiers marching about. But this was to be expected. Thomas French, who had visited Aden several times before, explained that Aden was important to the British, who originally took control of the port city to stop pirate attacks on passing British vessels headed to and from India. Over the years Aden had become an important stopping point for ships taking on coal and provisions.

Sam soon began to appreciate the efficient way the British ran things. His baggage was handled promptly through customs, and no one put out his hand expecting a bribe, or *basheesh*, as it was called, to stamp his passport. Sam helped Mr. French and his assistant, Alexander Maitland, through the customs and immigration process before hurrying to the roped-off area where he could see Jim Cantine waving at him. Sam and Jim shook hands, and Jim called a local boy over to carry Sam's bags.

Jim was brimming with information. "It's been challenging here," he began. "I hope you don't mind, but I've rented us a small house in Crater Town. It's a bit cramped but right in the thick of things. I can't wait until you meet Mr. Brunton, an agent of the British and Foreign Bible Society. He's been very kind to me. I've also been over to visit Reverend Gardner at the Scottish Mission at Sheikh Othman. He has a very interesting setup, and he took me to see Ion Keith-Falconer's gravesite."

"Do you think the Arabian Mission could take root here?" Sam asked.

Jim grimaced. "I'm not sure. I've been talking to Mr. Brunton about it and praying as I walk around. The big problem is the British presence here. They have everything sewn up. Nothing happens without their permission, and they say it's nearly impossible to get permission to travel inland. British checkpoints are set up on every road out of Aden. Besides that, a good percentage of the people here are from Somalia. I think we want to concentrate more on the local Arab population, don't you?"

Sam nodded, a little distracted by a passing young boy bent nearly horizontal carrying what looked like an impossibly high pile of dates on his back. Then he said, "We'll have to see. In the meantime we should learn all we can from the missionaries here and keep up with our language studies." He wanted to add, "and avoid catching malaria," thinking of how Ion had survived only ten months after setting foot in Aden, but he didn't. Sam knew that he had come to Arabia to labor, and to die if necessary. It was part of the commitment he had made when he signed the Student Volunteer Movement pledge four years before, and he had never doubted the ultimate price he might be asked to pay for doing so.

"Do you have any mail with you?" Jim asked.

"No," Sam replied. "Nothing caught up with me while I was in Cairo. Have you had any news of home?"

"No news, but I wrote to Kamil to see whether he would be willing to join us," Jim said. "I think he could start work among the Bedouins immediately, and we could support his efforts and learn from him. What do you think?"

"It sounds like a great idea," Sam replied. "Of course, I haven't met him, but everything you've told me makes me think he would be a great partner for our work. I hope he can come."

That afternoon the two young Americans set out to see the rest of Aden.

"This place is amazing," Jim said as they walked along. "The history is unbelievable. There are layers and layers of history under these buildings. Some say it is the place where Cain and Abel were buried, and there are seven Jewish synagogues here. The Jews have been in and around Aden for hundreds of years. Many of them are gifted artisans and craftsmen."

Sam and Jim wound their way through the streets of Crater Town. The city of Aden was built around a dormant volcano that formed a peninsula connected to the mainland by an isthmus. Crater Town was so named because it was located in the crater of the old volcano. Sam and Jim walked up to the northeastern wall of the crater, where steps were cut directly into the black rock.

"Are you up for a climb?" Jim asked. "This leads up to Jebel Shem-San, the highest point in Aden. It's a zigzagging path to the top, where there's a signal station for the shipping. It's quite a climb, but from up there you get a wonderful view of Steamer Point and the Gulf of Aden."

"Let's get going," Sam said with a smile. "There's nothing like a challenge!"

The two men climbed up the steep crater slope, slipping on the sand and lava fragments. They stopped several times to catch their breath before reaching the top. As Jim had promised, the view was magnificent. Sam could see the various areas of Aden stretched out below. Across the harbor he could see the barren hills of the mainland.

Jim pointed. "You can see what a wonderful port Aden is. The Arabs come across the desert with coffee, dates, spices, and wool to trade, and ships are passing by all the time. The British really needed this place to protect their ships from pirates and also because it's about midway between Zanzibar, Bombay, and

Cyprus in the Mediterranean, all of which the British control. It's the perfect refueling and provisioning station for ships coming and going through the Suez Canal."

"Yes, Mr. French told me as much as we were sailing into the harbor this morning," Sam said.

That night Sam could hardly sleep. When he relaxed and shut his eyes, he could still feel the rocking motion of the steamer. He heard unfamiliar noises, the rustling of insects on the grass mats on the floor, the howling of dogs, and the rhythmic marching of British guards patrolling the streets.

The next day there was more sightseeing to do. This time Jim took Sam to see one of the wonders of the ancient world—the Cisterns of Tawila. The cisterns were a series of tanks of varying shapes and capacities sculpted from the volcanic rock of Wadi Tawila, above Crater Town. Jim explained to Sam that the tanks were about two thousand years old, though no one knew for sure. By the time the British took control of Aden in 1839, the cisterns had fallen into disrepair. British engineers repaired and modified the tanks, which for years stored the water for Aden. Now the British were desalting seawater, and that's what most Europeans used. The locals got their water delivered by camel cart from inland wells.

Sam was impressed with the ingenious design of the cisterns and how they had been used over the centuries. He also had some new insight regarding water. He wrote to his father, "Living here, where it is so dry, certainly reminds me of how important water was in biblical days. When Jesus said he was the living water and anyone who thirsted could come to him and be satisfied, people hearing that would certainly have understood just how precious water was and what a wonderful gift Jesus was offering them."

Following their visit to the Cisterns of Tawila, Sam and Jim made their way to Sheikh Othman, just outside Aden, to visit the grave of Ion Keith-Falconer. Sam was deeply moved to be standing beside the grave of the young man whose life had helped get him thinking about Arabia as a mission field. Sam also thought about Ion's mother, whom he'd visited in Scotland months before. As he said a prayer for her, the words of Jesus from John 12:24 came to mind: "Unless a grain of wheat falls into the earth and dies, it remains alone; but if it dies, it bears much fruit" (RSV). Sam hoped that Ion's sacrifice would indeed bring much fruit in Arabia and that he might play a part bringing that about.

Less than two weeks after arriving in Aden, Sam was having grave doubts about whether he would live to see that fruit. He and Jim were both stricken with malaria, the same tropical disease that had claimed Ion's life. Sam's bones ached so badly it felt as though he were being beaten with a hammer, and his body shook uncontrollably. His only relief came when he faded out of consciousness. An English doctor attended Sam and Jim, spooning bitter quinine medicine down their throats and draping dampened sheets across their feverish skin.

After several days the worst of their symptoms began to subside. The doctor warned Sam and Jim,

"These bouts will come and go for years, you know. You will feel fine one day, and then, without warning, you will get a low fever and be useless for any work until it passes."

Sam nodded. In his private medical studies while attending New Brunswick Seminary, he had studied malaria and knew that what the doctor said was true. Once malaria got into your body, it never really left.

"Still," the doctor brightened up, "you have a lot to be grateful for. You are both going to recover, something I cannot say of all my malaria patients, even some as young and fit as the two of you."

Sam caught Jim's eye. He knew they were both thinking about Ion and how he had died just a few miles from where they now lay ill.

Both Sam and Jim were beginning to feel better when something happened that boosted their spirits. On February 7, 1891, Kamil arrived at their doorstep. He was ready and eager to begin his work with the Arabian Mission. Sam immediately realized what an asset Kamil would be. Kamil not only spoke flawless Arabic and English, but was also an excellent student of the Koran and the Old and New Testaments. He could compare and contrast the main ideas in these texts as succinctly as any theology professor Sam had ever listened to.

Kamil set to work immediately, walking out to where the caravans of Arabs gathered outside the city. As he engaged the camel drivers in conversation about Jesus, other drivers would stop what they were doing to listen and debate. In this way it was not uncommon for Kamil to attract a group of fifty to one hundred people, all listening to him proclaim the gospel and explain how it related to the Koran.

A month after Kamil's arrival, it became obvious to Sam and Jim that Aden would not make a good initial station for the Arabian Mission. The place was too small and under the thumb of the British. They decided to explore farther afield. Jim would stay in Aden, and Sam and Kamil would travel along the southern coast of Arabia to spy out the land. They set their sights on Makullah, a port town three hundred miles to the east along the coast.

The two men left Aden on board a sixty-foot sloop, or *saai*, named the *Mubarakat* (Blessed) on the evening of March 19, 1891. They were headed for Belhaf, which lay about three-quarters of the way to Makullah. In their luggage were 120 Arabic Bibles and New Testaments they had purchased from Mr. Brunton of the British and Foreign Bible Society. Sam and Kamil hoped to sell them along the way. The price was inexpensive, but selling the Bibles and New Testaments ensured that the buyers were serious about reading them. Sam and Kamil also carried with them a letter of introduction from a British officer in Aden to the local sultan at Makullah.

The *Mubarakat* had one short, heavy mast with a spar that supported a small sail. The sail was patched, and the sloop was rigged with palm leaf ropes. The sloop had no cabin, and since Sam and Kamil were the only first-class passengers, they got to sit in a canoe that had been hoisted aboard and wedged between bales of cotton and coffee.

Soon after setting out from Aden the crew started preparing dinner. It was the month of Ramadan, when Muslims fasted during the daytime, but the crew assured Sam they would cook for them during the day. As it turned out, neither Sam nor Kamil wanted food for the first twenty-four hours of the journey. During the night the wind kicked up and the waves rose, causing both of them seasickness. By the second day the men felt well enough to talk with the captain, the sailors, and their fellow passengers— twenty-five people in all. Everyone seemed willing to hear about the gospel, and by the third day two passengers had bought Bibles to read for themselves.

Sam marveled at how well Kamil could use the Koran to prove the Bible was true and how well his hearers responded to what he said. Kamil was always respectful and answered questions thoroughly. By the time they stopped at the village of Shefra for water supplies, the passengers were asking Kamil to read portions of the Bible aloud.

Kamil used the *tajweed*, a loud musical intoning required in Muslim recitation, when reading the Koran aloud. The passengers and crew listened with rapt attention and delight, and whenever Kamil paused, they shouted for him to continue.

On March 23, Sam and Kamil each took a group of sailors and spoke to them about the plan of salvation and how the prophecies of the Old Testament told of the coming of Jesus Christ. The sailors spoke among themselves and then said to Sam, "We can see that you are not infidels as we had previously believed

you were. You speak words of life that we understand." Afterward, whenever Kamil read Scripture
aloud the men would yell out, *"Zein, zein, wallah zein;
laisoo b'kuffar"* (Very fine; by the name of Allah, fine;
they are not infidels).

It was more than Sam could have hoped for. Both
the sailors and the passengers were open to the message he and Kamil sought to pass along.

Sam wondered if there were people living inland
from the coast and asked the captain about this.

"Yes, there are people," the captain said. "They
are like the sands that cannot be counted or num-
bered. Many sultans who are at perpetual war rule
them, and peace is secured in the end only by the aid
of the judges. There are no streams or rivers, and the
water is chiefly rainwater. There are some wells, but
they are scarce."

On Saturday, March 25, they sailed into Arkah, the
town of Sheikh Abdurahman el Badas and the site of
his tomb. The Arabs regarded the sheikh—an Islamic
elder—as a saint. Sam and Kamil got off the *Mubarakat* to stretch their legs and survey the town. They
had just strolled past a few houses when two men
walked up to them. Kamil spoke first. "Do you know
the gospel, and have you heard about the Christ?" he
asked.

"We have never heard of the Christ, nor do we
know what the gospel is," one of the men replied.
Kamil briefly explained the gospel as the two men
listened with deep interest. The men then invited the
missionaries to visit their home and tell them more.

Sam ran back to the boat to beg the captain to stay longer, but the captain refused. He explained that the harbor was unsafe to spend the night moored in and they needed to keep moving toward their destination. Sam was disappointed to leave Arkah, but he was also encouraged to know that people were open to the gospel.

On Monday, March 27, the *Mubarakat* sailed into Belhaf, the sloop's destination. Sam was sorry to say goodbye to the crew, who had bought six New Testaments between them.

Once on land, Sam needed to find a way to go the last eighty miles to Makullah. The local people wanted a lot of money to escort them by camel. No donkeys were available for sale or rent, and no other sloops were moored in the harbor. Eventually Sam bought passage on a twenty-seven-foot canoe, called a *flook*.

Only a captain and two sailors were aboard the canoe, and one of the sailors was assigned to bail out water before they even left the harbor. Sam talked to the captain and sailors about Christianity, and Kamil offered to read to them from the Gospel of John. The crew would have none of it. They spat and turned their heads away when Sam or Kamil tried to talk to them. The captain complained that he would have to scrub the entire boat out when the voyage was over, as "unclean" men were traveling in it. Sam and Kamil spent their time praying and reading the Bible silently as the vessel sailed on to Bir Ali, a small trading village with an excellent water supply.

Sam and Kamil left Bir Ali at dawn on March 29, and immediately Sam was concerned. The winds were stronger, and the waves were bigger than anything he'd experienced since arriving in Arabia. Soon the wind was howling, and each sailor clung to the side of the canoe with one arm while trying to bail out water with the other. Everything, including the luggage and precious Arabic Bibles, was drenched. Sam started to shiver. He was soaked to the skin, and the wind felt as if it were whipping right through him. He started singing hymns in English, and Kamil joined in. Then, as the waves grew higher than palm trees, the two men yelled encouragements to each other.

Sam was suddenly aware that the captain was yelling at them. "We are running ashore until the storm has passed. We cannot outrun it!"

Sam nodded vigorously as the two sailors grabbed the oars and began the difficult job of bringing the vessel about. It was some time before Sam felt the scraping of sand against the hull. The sailors jumped out—half swimming, half walking—and began dragging the boat to the beach. It proved too much of a struggle, and Sam and Kamil jumped into the sea. They gripped the canoe and helped to pull it toward land. The men finally managed to draw the boat up onto the beach to safety.

It felt wonderful to be on land again, but Sam noticed that the captain looked nervous. The captain's eyes kept darting from side to side as if he were expecting to see something. Just then a Bedouin man carrying a long spear appeared. It was so sudden that Sam wondered if he had been there all along.

The Bedouin saluted the men, who saluted back. Then he turned to Kamil and said, "You better not stop in this wilderness. It is full of godless Bedouins who will kill you or rob you of everything."

Kamil drew himself up to his full height and replied, "We fear nothing, for God is with us and we are His disciples. 'If God be for us, who can be against us?'"

The man grunted and disappeared as quickly as he had appeared.

"We haven't seen the last of him," the captain said grimly. "Mark my words. He's a scout. They'll have their hearts set on our boat and all of the luggage. We might have been better off taking our chances in the sea."

Five minutes later Sam saw one shadowy figure through the rain, then another. Both were armed with spears and arrows.

Chapter 8

Our Hearts Are Changed

Sam stood motionless and watched as two grim-faced men, spears drawn back over their shoulders, walked purposefully toward the boat. When the men were close enough for Sam to see the patterns woven into their robes, they stopped and saluted. Sam smiled and saluted back, as did Kamil. The captain and the rest of the crew stood still as statues rooted to the sand.

"We want coffee. You must give us coffee as rent for the land you are standing on. It is our land, and you have no right to be here," one of the men said.

There was a long silence. Sam waited for the captain to step forward, but he did not.

"We want coffee. Give us coffee," the Bedouin repeated. This time he had a harsh edge to his voice.

Sam decided that he had better say something, since it appeared no one else would. "We won't give you coffee, but you are welcome to some of our dates."

"No! Coffee!" the second man said, pointing his spear at Kamil. "Coffee!"

"No," Sam replied, looking the man in the eye.

There was another long pause.

"We do not want your dates. If you won't give us your coffee, we will take your money. You must pay rent. Do you understand? You are trespassing on our land. If you want safe passage you must pay us money."

Sam shook his head. "No money," he said. Just then out of the corner of his eye he noticed movement. Within seconds a crowd of Bedouin women and children surrounded them. They swarmed like bees, grabbing at the men's clothing, slipping their hands into the food sacks, and pulling at the boat. There were too many of them to stop, and Sam knew they must act quickly or they would be stripped of everything they had. He looked at Kamil and decided that he must be thinking the same thing.

Kamil drew a deep breath and called out, "We will not give money, but you had better think twice before attacking us. The captain has a gun that could kill five or six of you in the twinkling of an eye. If we fight each other, some of you and some of us will surely die. I am not worried for myself, for I have something here in my heart that will preserve me, for my conscience rests on the Lord Jesus Christ. But what will become of you?"

Sam waited to see what response this would bring, but it was as though the Bedouins had not heard Kamil's words. A group of women seized the boat and started to chant, "We will not let you go, we will not let you go."

Sensing that this was the moment to take charge, Sam pulled out his pocketknife, opened it, and walked up to the chief Bedouin. As he looked the man in the eye, he reached out and cut off a piece of beadwork that hung from the man's neck. "This is to remember you by, my friend," he said.

The Bedouin looked confused, and everyone fell silent.

"In exchange for these beads I have medicine in this boat that I will give you and explain to you how it can treat your ailments, but first we must deal with these," Sam continued, grabbing hold of the man's spear and sticking it tip-down into the sand. Kamil did the same with the other man's spear and then began to pray aloud. The women and children stopped what they were doing and listened. "God, O God of the universe, who made every grain of sand upon which we stand . . ." Kamil prayed using the Muslim style of prayer as he went on to talk about creation, Moses, the coming of Christ, and the power of the Holy Spirit.

As Sam surveyed the scene, it was as if someone had put a spell on the Bedouins. No one moved as Kamil prayed. After half an hour, Kamil concluded, "In the name and for the honor of the Lord Jesus Christ, our Redeemer and our Savior."

All of the Bedouins responded together, "Amen and amen." One of the men then exclaimed, "Our hearts are changed. Never again in our lives will we cut off the roads, rob on the highway, or speak harshly to a stranger."

"We will depart now," Sam said with authority.

The Bedouins stepped back to make way for Sam and Kamil to get to the boat, saying, "Ma-es-Salameh. Go in peace. May God preserve you."

The storm was still raging as the captain and sailors pushed the flook back into the ocean. Everyone climbed in, and the boat began to float away from the beach. The captain turned the rudder and pointed the boat back in the direction from which they had come.

"We are truly water in water," Kamil yelled to Sam over the noise of the wind and waves. Sam nodded and prayed silently that the captain would have the wisdom to make the best decision as to what to do next.

"We are going back to Bir Ali," the captain announced. "We will not make it to Makullah in these conditions." Then he added, "You are our brothers. If anything happens, we will give our lives for you."

Even though Sam knew the flook was still in danger of sinking, he sat quietly, filled with astonishment and joy. He could hardly believe the scene he had just experienced. It felt like something right out of the Book of Acts. As long as he lived, he was sure he would remember Kamil's prayer.

"Sharks! Look! To the left!" Kamil yelled, breaking into Sam's thoughts. Sam looked to his left. Sure enough, amidst the swirling white foam he caught sight of a triangular fin.

"Do not worry," one of the sailors yelled. He felt around in the bottom of the canoe with one hand and triumphantly produced a small drum. "This shark drum line will keep them away," he said, thumping it with the palm of his hand.

Sam smiled weakly. He had far more faith in God to protect them than he did in a drum line.

The boat made it back to Bir Ali safely. Sam and Kamil found lodging and dried out their wet clothing. Thankfully, the Bibles and New Testaments were unharmed. They had been well wrapped in oilskin, and although the covers were damp, the books' pages were dry.

Once they were warm and dry, Sam and Kamil discussed their options. Since neither one wanted to get back into another flook, they prayed that a larger boat would sail into port. And it did. The following day they found a large vessel bound for Makullah bobbing in the harbor at Bir Ali. Sam and Kamil quickly made friends with the captain and learned that he and the forty sailors aboard were from Muscat on the Gulf of Oman and were making their way home.

By Thursday morning word had spread that two Christians were aboard ship, and Sam found himself surrounded by sailors who wanted medicine for various ailments. As Sam attended to their needs, Kamil drew out a Koran and began to show the sailors that the Koran, the Torah (Old Testament), and the Injeel (the New Testament) were the books of God. Sam listened as best he could. He was always intrigued to hear how clearly Kamil made the connections between the Koran and the two Christian texts.

Every morning and evening and before each meal while they were aboard, Sam and Kamil prayed aloud, knowing that the crew were listening. Before the prayer Kamil always read a portion from the Gospels in the tajweed tone used in reading the Koran. This delighted the crew, who soon tried to outdo each other in being helpful to their two Christian passengers.

On Friday, two of the sailors came to Kamil and asked him to write out the prayers that he and Sam prayed aloud. They told Kamil that they liked his Christian prayers better than their own. Kamil wrote out the Lord's Prayer for them.

During the next two days of the voyage, Sam overheard the sailors talking to each other about the gospel. "Of a truth these are good men, and their doctrine is light upon light. We must act on what we have heard." And the crew did act. Before the vessel reached Makullah, they had bought thirty Bibles and New Testaments and assured the two missionaries that they would read them. Sam was overcome with joy.

When the ship reached Makullah, the crew begged Sam and Kamil to sail on with them to Muscat. Sam promised to follow later if it was possible. The sailors had tears in their eyes as they hugged Sam and Kamil goodbye.

With their letter of introduction in hand, Sam and Kamil visited the local sultan, who welcomed the men warmly into his sprawling palace on the waterfront. The sultan offered to lend them a house for as long as they wanted. Two of the sultan's servants carried their belongings to the house. Then it was time for Sam and Kamil to explore.

Makullah was a well-established town of about seven thousand people. It had finely paved streets lined with large houses, some four and five stories high. The town also had elaborate mosques but no Jewish synagogues or Christian churches. To the right of the town was a large Bedouin encampment clustered around a well.

Just after Sam and Kamil had settled into the house, the local people started knocking on the door. Word had quickly circulated that Sam had medical supplies. Sam set up a makeshift dispensary in the kitchen and began seeing patients. While Sam treated patients, Kamil talked to those waiting their turn about Christianity and offered Bibles for sale.

All went well until the following day when three local boys bought Bibles. In their excitement they took the Bibles to their schoolteacher and asked if they could study the Bible together. The teacher was furious and ordered the boys to burn the Bibles immediately. One of the boys ran back to Sam and Kamil to ask them what to do. Kamil suggested that the teacher come and speak with him.

Some tense moments passed as the two missionaries waited to see what would happen next. Would the town turn against them? The teacher did come to the house and brought two other teachers with him. Sam and Kamil greeted them with courtesy and kindness. After introductions, Kamil invited the teachers to sit. He then said, "Honored teachers, I have called you to take counsel and ask you about a very important matter and to tell you something new. If you find it to be true, help me to carry it out. If it be not true, teach me a better way, and if it be a true way, I will be very much obliged to you."

Sam tried not to let his smile show. He was impressed by the wise way Kamil approached hostile people.

The teachers replied respectfully, "Speak. We are your hearers."

"Thank you for your kindness," Kamil continued. "I would like to read to you from the Koran." With that he opened a Koran and began to read. The three teachers seemed delighted at how well he read.

When he had finished, Kamil said, "You will be pleased to know that my father, my grandfather, my great-grandfather, and many more generations back were all Muslims. My father completed a Mecca pilgrimage three times, my brothers have all been on the pilgrimage, and I am not an infidel. This is because I read the Torah and the Injeel. The Koran commands me to read those holy books with reverence and for inspiration. You do not believe me? Hear this."

Kamil opened the Koran again and read several more passages aloud. He then asked, "Does this Koran speak truth or falsehood?"

"Allah forbid that it should speak falsehood," one teacher said while the other two nodded in agreement.

"Are my words true? Does not the Koran encourage the reading of the Jewish and Christian scriptures?" Kamil asked.

"Yes," the teachers replied, "there is no doubting it."

"Then," Kamil said, "why did you forbid the boys to study the books?"

"We did not," one of the teachers said. "We would never do such a thing! Look, we will buy some of them for ourselves and read them." With that the three teachers took money from their pockets, and each purchased a Bible.

Sam was amazed. Once again he felt as though he were in the Book of Acts watching a miracle unfold.

The three teachers left the house happy, and before long the boys returned and brought their school friends to buy Bibles. "Our teachers told us we will study these together," they explained.

The following day, Sam was asked to go to the home of a man who was very ill with a large tumor in his stomach. Sam tapped into the tumor and drew off the watery liquid inside it. With the pressure released, the patient felt better immediately. Sam and Kamil knelt beside the man's bed. As they prayed for him in the name of Jesus Christ, men and children crowded around to hear their prayer. They all responded aloud with "amen" at the end of each sentence. Before Sam and Kamil left the house, the

owner bought a Bible from them and thanked God
for the opportunity to own it.

Many more residents of Makullah invited Sam
and Kamil into their homes. At each house the men
visited, Kamil read the Lord's Prayer and then sang
hymns. At the close of their prayers, the residents of
the house would respond with a chorus of "amen."

Time passed quickly, and on Tuesday, April 7,
1891, Sam and Kamil boarded a ship to return to
Aden. The Sultan insisted on paying for their passage
and food, and Sam promised the people of Makullah
that they would return one day. Amazingly, the trip
straight back to Aden took just four days. Sam spent
much of that time writing notes about what he had
learned.

Sam and Kamil reached Aden and were delighted
to find Jim in good health. Jim was amazed to learn
that the men had sold 110 copies of the Scriptures in
Arabic on their journey. He was especially interested
in the sailors' invitation to visit Muscat. Perhaps, the
three young men concluded, they should see more of
Arabia before deciding where God wanted them to
plant the Arabian Mission.

Chapter 9

Settling In

Ten weeks after arriving back in Aden, Sam set off on another missionary adventure—to the ancient city of Sana'a. This time he traveled alone since Kamil had gone to East Africa with a colporteur for the British and Foreign Bible Society. Jim was traveling around the coast of the Arabian Peninsula to Muscat to learn more about the possibilities of missionary work there.

On June 27, Sam steamed out of Aden harbor aboard the *Tuna*. The vessel headed west, through the straits of Bab-el-Mandeb. It then headed up the Red Sea back to Al Hudaydah, which Sam had visited on his way to Aden from Suez. Al Hudaydah was about one hundred miles west of Sana'a. Sam intended to apply to the Turkish authorities for a permit to travel across Yemen to Sana'a. When he arrived in Al Hudaydah, he realized that this was not possible.

The situation in Sana'a, Sam learned, was tense. Two ships filled with Turkish troops had arrived and were disembarking, on their way to reinforce two thousand Turkish soldiers occupying Sana'a as part of the Ottoman Empire. Six thousand Bedouins were said to be waiting in the mountains outside the city for the right time to attack. Indeed, there had been war in and around Sana'a for months as the Bedouin tribes tried to fight back against their oppressive Ottoman rulers. The Italian consul in Al Hudaydah told Sam the Turkish authorities would not issue a permit to travel inland. Without alternative options, Sam decided to hire a mule and driver and set off without permission.

Sana'a would be the farthest inland Sam had traveled on the Arabian Peninsula, and he was eager to view its interior. He spent most of the six-day journey on the back of a mule. What he saw fascinated him. Unlike most areas of the world that were lush at the coast and more barren or desertlike in the interior, the countryside on the coast around Al Hudaydah was rocky and barren, although the land became greener and more fertile farther inland. The mountainsides were being cultivated to grow coffee, millet, and grapes and other fruit. Hundreds of camels, cows, and sheep grazed in the green valleys. The scenery was more like what Sam would have expected to see in England than in Arabia.

The temperature had a lot to do with the changes Sam saw. When Sam left Al Hudaydah, the temperature had been nearly one hundred degrees Fahrenheit. As the mule train climbed ever higher on the way inland, however, the temperature began to drop. By the time Sam reached Sana'a, over seven thousand feet above sea level, the temperature was eighty degrees during the day and fell to near sixty at night.

As Sam approached Sana'a, he could not help but imagine himself to be back in Bible times. There seemed to be almost nothing modern around to remind him that he was in the nineteenth century. Sana'a itself was one of the oldest continuously inhabited cities in the world. Sam had read that according to popular legend, Shem, the son of Noah, had founded the city.

The Italian consul in Al Hudaydah had given Sam the address of an Italian merchant in Sana'a, and Sam made his way through the narrow, winding streets to the house. It was like walking through a maze. The mud-brick houses decorated with white geometric shapes rose three or four stories high on both sides of the street. Sam found the house he was looking for, and the merchant agreed to let him stay for one night only. The merchant explained that it might offend the local government if he were seen entertaining an American missionary.

Sam accepted the offer and set about exploring Sana'a. He soon found himself on the edge of the old fortified city, surrounded by ancient clay walls about thirty-five feet high. As he made his way through the thousand-year-old Yemen Gate into the old city, he marveled at the houses. Unlike any he had seen in

Aden or even in Al Hudaydah, they were tall and narrow and decorated with elaborate frescoes and stained-glass windows. Mosques seemed to be everywhere in the old city. None was more impressive than the thirteen-hundred-year-old Great Mosque of Sana'a, with its towering minaret. The streets of Sana'a thronged with people. Numerous markets sold bread, spices, raisins, cotton, copper, pottery, and silverware.

Sam spent a comfortable night with his Italian merchant host. The next day he went to a *kahwah* (coffee shop) to inquire about finding another place to stay. One of the men at the coffee shop offered Sam a room. Sam gratefully accepted. During the night, Turkish officers came to the house and demanded Sam's passport. They told Sam he would have to pay a fee to have it returned. Sam had expected this, and after he paid the fee, his passport was returned to him.

Following this experience, Sam decided that it was better to work *with* the Turks than against them. Before leaving Aden for East Africa, Kamil had given Sam the name of a friend in Sana'a who was a Turkish army officer. Sam decided it was a good time to pay the officer a visit.

The Turkish officer turned out to be friendly and helpful. He listened with interest as Sam described his adventure so far, and he invited Sam to stay at his home. But that lasted only one night. The next day the officer received a letter from his superior officer. The letter stated that given the present state of the country and the danger from war, it was undesirable for a Turkish officer to entertain an American missionary in his house. Sam returned to the kahwah to find another room to rent.

Sam's presence in Sana'a drew attention, and a small crowd followed him wherever he went. He realized that it was too dangerous to speak openly about Christianity out of doors, but Sam felt safe reading chapters from the Gospel of John to the men curious enough to venture into his rented room. He even sold a few copies of the Gospel of John and gave away a half dozen others to Arabs in Sana'a. He was pleased that every person who received a copy was grateful. One old sheikh even kissed the New Testament Sam gave to him.

One of the more interesting areas Sam wandered around was the Jewish section of Sana'a. Sam was surprised to learn that Jews had lived in Sana'a for centuries and existed happily side by side with the Muslim population of the city.

After a week in Sana'a, Sam decided to return to Aden. Given the presence of so many Turkish troops and the constant threat of war, he didn't think Sana'a was a good place to start the mission.

Back in Al Hudaydah Sam boarded a steamer bound for Aden. Several British military officers and government officials were aboard ship on their way to Bombay, India. As the ship steamed down the Red Sea, Sam told the men he was on his way back from an expedition to Sana'a. At first the British officials didn't believe him. "You don't just wander into Sana'a. It's nearly impossible to get a visa to visit there," one of the officials declared. Another added, "I don't know a single white person who has ever set foot in the place. It takes years to get permission to go there."

As Sam described the things he had seen in Sana'a and showed them the pictures he had sketched, the British officials eventually believed his story. "That's extraordinary," one of the officials told him. "You should write up your observations and apply to become a fellow of the Royal Geographic Society. With your kind of adventurous spirit, they would love to have you."

At first Sam laughed at the idea—and at the application fee of twenty pounds. But the more he thought about it, the more he liked the notion. Who could tell what doors being a member of the Royal Geographic Society might open for him in Arabia and even at home in the United States?

Back in Aden, Sam found himself alone. Kamil was still in East Africa, and Jim had not yet returned from Muscat, though he had sent Sam a letter. When he opened the letter, Sam was surprised to learn that Jim was not in Muscat but in Basrah, at the northern end of the Persian Gulf. According to Jim, an Irish doctor and his wife had heard that two young Americans were looking for a place to start a mission and had sent a letter inviting him to visit them in Basrah. Jim wrote that he was impressed by what he had seen of Basrah. He urged Sam to join him there.

The letter also contained some sad news. While he was in Muscat, Jim had learned that Thomas Valpy

French had died of heatstroke shortly after arriving there. Although Sam had gotten to know the bishop only recently, the man's tenacity and focus on sharing the gospel with Muslims had left an indelible imprint.

Sam made all the necessary arrangements and set sail for Basrah on October 1. To get to his destination, he had to sail to Karachi, Pakistan, and change to a steamer headed for ports in the Persian Gulf. On October 18 the ship stopped for a day at Muscat, on the southwestern edge of the Arabian Peninsula. Sam used the occasion to visit the grave of Thomas Valpy French at Cemetery Cove.

From Muscat the steamer sailed in a northwesterly direction across the Gulf of Oman, through the Strait of Hormuz, and then over five hundred miles up to the end of the Persian Gulf. It entered Shatt-el-Arab (River of the Arabs) and sailed sixty miles upstream to Basrah, where Sam arrived on October 26.

Basrah was situated just below the confluence of the Tigris and the Euphrates Rivers. It had a population of about sixty thousand and was loosely controlled by the Turks. The area was famous for the dates it produced, and groves of date palms surrounded the city. Upriver from Basrah was the location of Ur of the Chaldeans, from which God had told Abraham to set out on his journey.

Sam was glad to see Jim again, and he appreciated the hospitality of Dr. Marcus Eustace and his wife. The house the Eustaces were renting was large and comfortable and felt to Sam more like home than anything he had experienced so far in Arabia. As Jim showed Sam around Basrah, the two of them prayed that God would either open or close the door for them to work in the city.

Dr. Eustace showed Sam the spot where he envisioned a large mission hospital. Sam liked the idea. His experience in Arabia had already shown him how much more open the local people were to the gospel when they were receiving medical attention. Within a week of Sam's arrival in Basrah, Sam and Jim both felt confident that this was the place to start. The Arabian Mission now had a home.

Sam and Jim were excited to feel that they were finally putting down roots. Once they made the decision, they had much to do. They soon decided that Sam should return to Aden to pack a few belongings he and Jim had there and, they hoped, persuade Kamil to join them in Basrah.

On November 15, 1891, Sam set sail for Aden. Good news greeted him when he arrived. The first piece of good news was a letter from the United States. The home committee of the Arabian Mission had approved two new missionaries to come and work with them. One was a doctor, and the other was Sam's younger brother Peter. As well, Kamil had returned from East Africa. When he learned of the plan to establish a mission station in Basrah, he was eager to join Sam and Jim there. Sam sent him on ahead to join Jim.

After Sam had taken care of everything in Aden, he returned to Basrah in January. When he arrived, more good news awaited. While Sam was in Aden, Jim had traveled north to Baghdad to visit the Church Missionary Society (CMS) missionaries there. The outstation was ten years old, and the missionaries had already established a school and hospital and had helped to man a British and Foreign Bible Society Bible distribution center. Even though the CMS worked among the old Christian sects rather than Muslims, Sam was excited to hear about their methods and experiences. It pleased him to know that the CMS missionaries in Baghdad had decided to send three Christians, who were colporteurs for the British and Foreign Bible Society, to work with them in Basrah.

By mid-March, Sam felt confident that the Arabian Mission was settling in to take on the work at Basrah. The team consisted of Sam, Jim, Kamil, and three Bible Society colporteurs. This was more than enough to run a Bible shop, begin systematic one-on-one evangelism, and plan for the possibility of a hospital. Dr. Eustace was enthusiastic about heading up that effort.

Things did not go as planned. The first blow came when Marcus Eustace announced that he and his wife had decided to rejoin the CMS mission work in Persia and were being stationed in the Afghan frontier. Sam and Jim were sorry to hear the news, but knew that a doctor was on the way from the United States to join their work. They were relieved when Dr. Clarence Riggs reached Basrah.

Things did not go well with the new recruit from the start. Dr. Riggs argued with Sam and Jim about religious matters and shook his head when Jim requested he ask a blessing at the table. Later, when the question of leading their morning devotions came up, Clarence said courteously, "I have never done anything like that, and I am not about to start now. You can call upon me for any medical services, but anything of religious nature is quite out of my line."

Neither Sam nor Jim said anything more at the time, but a week or so later, Clarence cornered them. "Why is it that the two of you seem to have more in common with each other than you do with me? After all, we're all Americans."

"Why, doctor," Sam replied, "isn't that unavoidable? You don't believe in what we are trying to do for the Arabs. You don't believe as we do about God."

"How could I?" the doctor replied indignantly. "You seem to believe that God came down from heaven and became a little babe. No one believes that nowadays."

Despite the difficulties with Clarence, the work continued. The doctor was happy to open a small medical clinic in the house Dr. Eustace had rented, and the colporteurs opened a Bible shop in the bazaar. Kamil was becoming an effective and well-recognized man about town. He and Sam often sat together in the coffee shops, talking to others about the real meaning of the Christian message and how it differed from the message of their prophet Mohammed.

When writing a report on the missionaries' work in Basrah to send home to the United States, Sam reflected on how much they had accomplished in the first quarter of the year. There had been bumps along the way, and Clarence was getting more unpredictable every day. But all in all, things were moving ahead. As he mailed his report, Sam had no way of knowing what lay ahead for the missionary band in Basrah before the letter even reached America.

Chapter 10

Hope and Disappointment

On May 28, 1892, Sam set out for the nearby village of Majil. He'd been there once before and had talked to several Muslim men who were open to discussing the Bible. He took Kamil along with him on this trip. When they arrived at Majil, the two men received a warm welcome. It seemed that every man in the village was present to welcome them back. The village men beckoned for Sam and Kamil to stand under the shade of a large date palm and talk to them about God's love.

Sam was happy to do so. He stepped forward, opened the Gospel of John, and read chapter three, verse sixteen: "For God so loved the world, that he gave his only begotten Son, that whosoever believeth in him should not perish, but have everlasting life."

As Sam began to talk about the meaning of the verse, one or another of the village men occasionally interrupted him with a question. Sam and Kamil took turns answering the questions.

When Sam finished speaking, the crowd would not leave—they wanted to hear more. Sam gave copies of the Gospel of John to those who could read and follow along as Kamil read several chapters from it. Sam marveled. It was like a giant open-air Sunday school class back home. Forty or fifty people listened carefully as the Gospel of John was read to them. When Kamil finished reading, Sam asked the group if they thought the words they had heard were true.

"Yes, this is true," several of the men replied.

Sam then explained in clear, simple language that all men are sinners in the sight of God and that "without the shedding of blood there is no forgiveness of sins" (Hebrews 9:22 RSV). He then told his audience that the blood of Christ, shed on the "wood of the cross" was the only means by which to atone for their sin. When he had finished explaining, he again asked, "Is what you have heard true?"

Several men spoke for the group. "Some things are true, and other things are true, but we do not believe them."

Sam smiled and replied, "Think over all you have heard. We will come back again and answer your questions."

The men escorted Sam and Kamil to the edge of their village, where Sam prayed for them all. "Come back next month," they said. "You speak words that interest us."

As they made their way back along the hot, dusty road to Basrah, Sam and Kamil prayed for the men of the village. They had been allowed to preach and answer questions about Christianity for three and a half hours. This was a hopeful sign.

Back in Basrah, it soon became clear to Sam and Jim that the local authorities were not happy with their activities. The lease on the house Dr. Eustice had originally rented was about to expire, and because they now ran their small medical clinic there, they needed to find new accommodations. Sam and Jim found a less expensive house and asked if they could rent the place. At first the owner said yes, but then he changed his mind, telling them that he might move into the house himself. They looked again, but each inquiry about renting a place ended with the same result. For some reason the owner would not rent the house to them. Sam asked an Arab friend why it was so difficult for them, even when they offered to pay more for the place than the going rate. The friend replied, "Don't you know? The governor has posted notices that under severe penalties no one in the city is allowed to rent a house to the American missionaries." Sam's heart dropped. He knew this was serious. In Basrah the authority of the governor was absolute.

Even if they were sympathetic and interested in helping the missionaries, the few English business-men residing in the city were in no position to antag-onize the local authorities. It seemed to Sam that the one thing they could do to secure a new place to rent was to pray about the situation.

Later that week, Sam visited the Persian consul in Basrah. The consul was suffering from a hacking cough, and Sam gave him some medicine to help relieve his symptoms. The Persian consul was so grateful that he asked if there was anything he could do for Sam in return. In a moment of inspiration, Sam explained how no one in town would rent them a house because the governor had forbidden them to do so.

The consul laughed when he heard this. "The only person in this whole town he cannot intimidate is me! I have an empty house, much better than the one you are in, which you can have at the same rent you now pay. You can move right in. The governor will not dare to say a word to me."

Sam could hardly wait to tell Jim the good news of how God had answered their prayers. However, Sam and Jim were still aware that many rich and powerful men in Basrah did not want them there, and they wondered what else those men might do to run them out of town.

Disaster struck on Friday, June 24, 1892. Sam's day had been a busy one. It started early in the morning when he conducted the funeral of a carpenter who had been a crewman on board a foreign steamer. Following the funeral service Sam hurried home to take care of Clarence, who was ill with a high fever. At lunchtime Jim arrived at the house and announced that Kamil had fallen ill with vomiting and diarrhea. Sam sent a helper ahead with medicine for Kamil. At five o'clock in the afternoon, he left Clarence's side and set out to walk the two miles to the room where Kamil was staying. He had gone only a mile when Jakoob Yohanna, a native Christian colporteur, met him on the road and said, "Sir, I hate to bring you bad news. Kamil is dead!"

Sam stood motionless, trying to absorb what he had just heard. Kamil, dead? Was that possible? Sam ran the second mile to Kamil's room and found it overflowing with Turkish soldiers and Muslim religious leaders. Sam wondered how they had gotten there so quickly. He stood at the door and watched. The soldiers were rifling through Kamil's papers while the mullahs were busy praying Muslim prayers over his body, which they were washing with a mixture of camphor and water. A pungent smell filled the room.

"Stop that," Sam said in a loud voice. "Everyone in this room knows that Kamil was a Christian. There are many witnesses to the fact. He should have Christian prayers said over him. He would not want Muslim rituals performed. He lived as a Christian, and he would want to die as one."

"We have no way of knowing that," one of the Turkish soldiers replied.

"Of course you do!" Sam said. "Look at the books on the table. What do you see? They are Bibles and Christian religious books. Read any page from Kamil's diary that you are holding, sir. It will bear witness to the fact that Kamil was a Christian missionary."

"We do not have time to read," the soldier answered. "When a Muslim dies, the prayers must begin immediately."

The chanting and washing continued. "God is Great. Holiness to thee, oh God, and to thee be praise. Great is thy Name. Great is thy greatness. Great is thy praise. There is no deity but thee. O God, those whom thou dost keep alive amongst us keep alive in Islam, and those whom thou causest to die let them die in the faith."

Just then Jim arrived. His face turned white as he assessed the situation. "How did this happen?" he asked. " Kamil was a strong, young man."

Sam shook his head and whispered to his coworker, "I don't know. They are trying to bury him immediately as a Muslim. I suspect foul play. There needs to be an autopsy. Do you think he might have been poisoned?"

"Something is very wrong here," Jim agreed. "How did all these men get here so fast? Why is this so important to them?"

Sam took a deep breath. He knew he had to lay aside the shock he was feeling at Kamil's sudden death and do whatever he could to get to the bottom of the situation before Kamil's body was carried away and buried. He was sorry that Clarence was too ill to come and perform an autopsy. He wondered whether they could find anyone else who would tell them the truth.

After a few more minutes of arguing, Sam sensed that it was pointless to talk to the people in Kamil's room. "You stay here," he told Jim. "I'll try to get help from the Turkish authorities, and if they won't listen, I'll appeal to the British."

Sam rushed to the main office of the Turkish authorities in Basrah, but his efforts proved fruitless. He was told that it would take forty-eight hours to investigate the matter and decide what do to about it. By then any kind of funeral service, Christian or Muslim, would have been over.

It was 9:30 p.m. when Sam arrived at the home of the British consul. The consul was sympathetic to the situation but fretted about what he had the authority to do. After all, Sam was an American asking for help with the body of a man from Syria.

An hour later Jim tracked Sam down at the British consul's home. "It's too late," he announced. "The Muslims have performed their funeral rites and taken Kamil's body to be buried. They won't say where."

The British consul raised his hands in defeat. "That is the way it is here. I am sorry I could not help your friend. But perhaps there is one thing I can do. I will send a man back with you to his room to put the British consulate seal on the door. Perhaps that will ensure that his property is not carried away without your permission."

"Thank you," Sam replied.

Sam and Jim, accompanied by the man from the British consulate, made their way silently back to Kamil's room. There was nothing to say. Sam hoped that the seal of the British consulate would be respected, but it was not. Most of Kamil's books and diaries were taken away, and Sam was never able to discover where Kamil's body had been buried.

As the days passed, Sam and Jim came to believe that the Muslim religious men and the Turkish authorities had prior knowledge of Kamil's impending death. Sam and Jim researched Muslim law and discovered that a male apostate—a person who had left the Muslim faith he had been raised to believe—must be put to death. If the apostate was still a boy, he was to be imprisoned until he became a man and then killed by the sword. It was sobering information, especially since Kamil had received letters from his father threatening to ensure he was killed if he did not give up Christianity and return to the Muslim faith.

Sam and Jim realized they would never know whether or not Kamil had been poisoned. One thing they knew for sure: their most able Arabic speaker and evangelist was dead, and his death left a tremendous loss.

Soon after Kamil's death, two of the three colporteurs who had been sent from Baghdad to help the mission announced they were leaving. The first man planned to emigrate to the United States, while the second man returned to Baghdad to take care of family matters.

Although Clarence recovered from his illness, his relationship with Sam and Jim deteriorated until both sides wrote about their concerns to the home committee. Their answer was swift and final. Dr. Riggs was dismissed from the Arabian Mission. While this was a relief to Sam and Jim, it was also discouraging. Administering medical care was key in reaching the community with the gospel, and now their doctor was being forced to leave.

The only bright spot, as far as Sam was concerned, was the anticipated arrival of his brother Peter from the United States in December. But that was several months away. In the meantime, Sam decided to visit Baghdad.

Around Mesopotamia

Sam sat in a deck chair on the small steamer, wiping sweat from his brow as he surveyed the scene. He was headed up the Tigris River that stretched for nearly twelve hundred miles north to southeastern Turkey. It was mid-July, and he was glad to escape the stifling heat of Basrah and take up the CMS missionaries' invitation to visit them in Baghdad. Sam hoped to journey overland from Baghdad to the town of Hillah and complete the loop back to Basrah by taking another steamer down the Euphrates River. As he sat on deck, he picked up his journal, opened it, and wrote, "What is now the independent kingdom of Iraq was in those early days called by its old Bible name, 'the land between the rivers'—Mesopotamia."

As he looked out at the muddy river, Sam knew he was right in the middle of biblical history. The Tigris was one of the four rivers that flowed out of the Garden of Eden, and Daniel had received his vision on the banks of the river. Abraham dwelt in Mesopotamia as well, before traveling to Haran. Sam felt like one of the ancient prophets spying out the land, looking for towns and villages that might be future centers for missionary work. As he traveled up the river, he was able to speak to the passengers and crew and quietly distribute portions of Scripture to those who asked for them.

On July 25, 1892, Sam arrived in Baghdad and made his way to the home of Dr. and Mrs. Sutton of the CMS. The Suttons warmly welcomed him. Sam also visited Jakoob, the colporteur who had worked with them at the Arabian Mission in Basrah. Sam learned that Jakoob was now forbidden to travel outside the city because of his Christian activities. Nonetheless, Jakoob was determined to keep sharing his faith and had gathered several Muslim men inter-ested in Christianity with whom he read the Bible, answering their questions. Sam was impressed with Jakoob's zeal.

One of the Muslim men in the group was Oman, who happened to be visiting Jakoob at the same time as Sam. Oman was interested in learning more about Christianity and the gospel. When he learned of Sam's plans, he offered to accompany him on the journey to Hillah and then down the Euphrates to Basrah in exchange for the opportunity to study the

New Testament with Sam. Sam welcomed the suggestion and quickly hired two mules for the journey.

At four o'clock in the afternoon on July 27, two days after Sam arrived in Baghdad, he and Oman joined a group of Arabs, Persians, and Turks all bound for Hillah, about sixty miles south of Baghdad. Some in the group were merchants, while others were pilgrims headed to the sacred shrines in the holy city of Najaf, beyond Hillah.

Several women were traveling with the group, but they were not allowed any contact with the men. Sam felt sad for the women, knowing that they were hidden behind curtains in cagelike structures called *taht-i-vans* that dangled from either side of the camels. He thought about how difficult it must be for the women to travel this way, unable to stretch their legs or talk to anyone. The sight of the women in the taht-i-vans reminded Sam of how differently Muslim men treated women from the way Jesus cared for women. Muslim men did not consider women as equals and required that the women be hidden from sight.

A group of Muslim ascetics was also traveling in the caravan. Known as *dervishes* for their poverty and austerity, the group was recognizable by the bright green turbans they wore. To complete the caravan, several muleteers were leading pairs of mules with coffins strapped crosswise between them. The coffins contained the remains of Muslim believers who had wished to be buried in holy ground in Najaf.

As the caravan made its way south from Baghdad, there was little to see—just huge swaths of desert broken by mounds of earth under which lay remnants of ancient civilizations. Occasionally Sam saw a set of shining white camel bones strewn along the trail and picked clean by vultures.

The group traveled for only four hours in the 110-degree Fahrenheit heat before stopping to rest under the starry sky. At midnight they were off again, taking advantage of the cooler night air. The caravan did not stop until mid-morning, when the passengers took shelter in a public *khan*, or inn. The khan consisted of a large enclosure with heavy walls made of sun-dried bricks. It had a single entrance wide enough for heavily laden beasts up to the size of a camel to pass through. The center of the khan was a courtyard open to the sky. Along the interior of the khan's four walls were a number of alcoves, or niches, about ten feet long and six feet wide and raised four feet off the ground. The niches were resting places for those traveling in the caravan, and Sam and Oman sought out one to rest in.

From his niche, Sam surveyed the scene. In the center of the open courtyard were a well and a large prayer platform. As the khan filled and there were no more empty niches, people began to sleep on the platform. The rest of the courtyard was used to stack the baggage that the animals were carrying and for the animals to roam and rest. The keeper of the khan provided feed for the animals to eat and sold other food supplies to the travelers.

Before he slept, Sam had a conversation with the sheikh of the small village. The sheikh was an old man who sat surrounded by his greyhound dogs, which he explained he used to hunt gazelle. Sam was surprised to learn that herds of gazelle were in the area. He had seen no signs of animal life except for birds and the camel bones.

At midnight the caravan was off again. By now everyone in the group knew that Sam was a Christian, and several of the men engaged in lively conversations with him. In the quiet moments, Sam read the Bible to Oman and answered his questions.

After twelve hours of traveling that day, they reached the Euphrates River. The riverbank was fringed with thick groves of date palms—what a contrast to the barren and dusty land they had passed through! Sam paid a toll, and he and Oman were ferried across the river on a rickety raft to Hillah, where they rented a room in an inn.

The next day the pair toured the ruins of the ancient city of Babylon, four miles north of Hillah. Parts of the crumbling old city wall were still visible, and mounds of clay bricks that had once been houses and other city buildings were everywhere. While Babylon, long abandoned, was now just a pile of rubble, it still amazed Sam to be viewing a site that figured so largely in the Old Testament.

On July 31, 1892, Sam and Oman left Hillah and began the journey down the Euphrates, sailing in a native boat. The Euphrates River was muddier than the Tigris but less winding. The boat sailed downstream all night until it arrived at Diwaniyah the following afternoon. Along the way it passed villages on the riverbank. One of the Arab crewmen pointed out a site that was believed to be the tomb of Job.

Once he reached Diwaniyah, Sam was directed to the *serai*, or government house, where he was welcomed. The local *pasha*, an officer of high rank, invited Sam to join him for a meal and peppered him with questions while they ate. He wanted to know how the laws in the United States worked and whether Abraham Lincoln's son had seized power after his father was assassinated. Sam answered the questions as best he could, trying to remember how little he had once known about the culture of the Middle East.

The pasha warned Sam about the risk of piracy on the river south of Diwaniyah and advised him to hire two soldiers to protect the boat. Sam accepted the pasha's advice and hired Salim and Salad. The men hardly acted like soldiers, spending time patching their uniforms, sleeping in the bottom of the boat, and eating bread and dates. Still, Sam was beginning to understand that this was the way things were done in Arabia. Foreigners, particularly those who could be intimidated, were seen as an endless source of revenue for the local people.

As the boat continued south toward Samawah, Sam noticed there was more activity along the river's edge. Herds of large, black water buffalo swam across the river pursued by shouting, swimming, and swearing herdsmen. As night fell, the boat approached the town of Rumaythah, where a hundred tents were spread out beside the river as people gathered for a religious ceremony. The captain seemed worried about docking the boat for the night, but there was little he could do. The rapids ahead were too dangerous to be run by starlight.

The air was hot and sticky, and Sam didn't sleep much that night. He was wide awake when a group of local men rushed the boat armed with flintlock rifles and *mikwars*, heavy sticks knobbed with sandstone. Sam's heart raced as the two soldiers he had hired stepped forward with their guns drawn and talked to the local men. To Sam's great relief the local men left as quickly as they had come.

Early the next morning the boat set out from Rumaythah. Soon afterward they ran the rapids, which were shallow, and on several occasions the men had to get out and push the boat across the shallows. They made it safely through the rapids and reached Samawah, the next large town downstream, in about four hours. Since there was now less chance of piracy, Sam dismissed the two soldiers before going to secure quarters for the night.

It was the day before Ashura—the tenth day of the month of Muharram in the Islamic calendar—when Shia Muslims would gather to mourn the martyrdom of Mohammed's grandson, Hussein ibn Ali, at the Battle of Karbala in the year 680. All of the shops were closed, and the residents of the town were excitedly making arrangements for the next day's celebration. Sam was relieved and grateful to have found a room for rent overlooking the bazaar.

No sooner had Sam climbed the stairs to his room than a messenger arrived from the local governor.

"My master says you cannot leave your room under any circumstances. You are a foreigner here. Even the Sunni Muslims stay off the streets during Ashura. If you venture out, the governor will not be responsible for your safety. The people will become violent if a nonbeliever is among them at this time."

Sam took the warning seriously and spent the rest of the day resting and reading the Bible with Oman. Of the celebration that occurred the next day, Sam wrote in his journal, "[S]aw the confusion of . . . Ashura from the window, the tramp of a mob, the beating of breasts, the wailing of women, the bloody banners and mock martyr scenes, the rhythmic howling and cries of 'Ya Ali! Ya Hassan! Ya Hussein!' until throats were hoarse and hands hung heavy for a moment, only to go at it again."

The following day everything appeared to be quiet, and Sam was able to leave his room. He spoke to several other men staying at the inn and sold several portions of Scripture.

On August 4, Sam booked passage for himself and Oman in a *meheleh* (large riverboat) loaded with barley being transported to Basrah. The only available place for them aboard was a low cabin under the aft deck filled with boxes, old clothes, ropes, lanterns, and provisions. It was also the only place aboard that offered shelter from the blazing midday sun.

Below Samawah the Euphrates began to broaden and the riverbanks were lined with palms and willows. Then the river became silted and brown, and the meheleh could not pass over the muddy shallows without everyone getting into the water and lifting the vessel downstream.

On August 11 they arrived at Kuma, where the boat had to tie up for the night. By now Sam was eager to get back to Basrah. He hired a native paddler and canoe to take him and Oman the last miles down river to Basrah. They set off at dusk. The water was calm, giving Sam the opportunity to write in his journal: "Seven hundred miles of touring along populous rivers and historic ruins, seven hundred miles of Muslim empire awaiting the conquests of the cross, two missionaries at Basrah—what are these among so many? The Euphrates and Tigris are the natural highways for the gospel in North Arabia, even as the Nile is for that other land of the patriarchs, Egypt. And even so should they be occupied, village after village, by schools and gospel agencies."

Sam and Oman parted ways when the canoe reached Basrah. Oman had not become a Christian on the journey, as Sam had hoped he would, but he did understand the gospel and promised to continue reading the New Testament.

Now that Sam was back in Basrah, it was time to turn his attention to his next project—welcoming his brother Peter to the Arabian Mission.

Chapter 12

Bahrain

On December 7, 1892, Sam found himself aboard yet another boat, this time a slow gulf steamer headed for the island of Bahrain off the coast of the Arabian Peninsula, 350 miles south of Basrah. Once again he was on his way to "spy out the land" to see whether the island would be a good place to establish a mission station. He also had another motive for traveling to Bahrain: the steamer carrying his brother Peter would make a stop there, and Sam wanted to meet him and travel back to Basrah with him. It would give the two men time to catch up on all the family news before Peter began adjusting to life in Arabia.

Two days after the boat set out from Basrah, the island of Bahrain came into view, and Sam began to pray hard. He had been told it was difficult for a Christian missionary to land and stay on the island, much less speak openly about the gospel. Because there was not a dock large enough for the steamer in Manamah, the largest city on the island, it dropped anchor three miles offshore. Sam, along with other passengers and cargo, was ferried ashore in a smaller boat.

Sam was surprised when he encountered no difficulties with admittance onto the island. Still, he decided it might be a good idea to stay away from the waterfront until after the steamer had sailed on, lest anyone change his mind about his staying. He deposited his suitcase at the post office and set out on a brisk walk around town. He did not return to collect his suitcase until after he saw the smoke from the steamer's funnels disappear over the horizon. Now that he was safely on Bahrain, Sam set out to find somewhere to stay. He was able to rent a room adjoining a mosque, where he deposited his belongings. He then set out to explore more of Manamah, at the northern end of the thirty-four-mile-long by eleven-mile-wide island.

A week after arriving in Bahrain, Sam decided to explore the interior of the island. He hired a donkey and a guide and was soon riding through date palms and aloe groves on his way to Salmabad and the ruined Portuguese fort there. From the old fort he crossed pastureland and passed more stands of date palms before coming to A'ali, a larger village to the south. Stretching south and west of A'ali was a barren plain filled with rocks and curious sand-covered mounds, each about thirty or forty feet high. When Sam asked the guide what the mounds were, the guide replied that there had once been a great and wicked city of unbelievers there and that all of the inhabitants of the place had been turned to boulders.

From A'ali the road led southeast to Rifa Sharki and Rifa Gharbi, two large villages. On the way, Sam got to see some of Bahrain's native animals—great flamingoes, gazelles, desert rabbits, and even hedgehogs.

As they rode back along the coast to Manamah, the guide pointed out to Sam the oyster banks, where up to thirty thousand men would dive for pearls during the season from July to October. Bahraini pearls were the purest in the world because of the fresh-water springs that flowed under the ocean around the oyster beds. The guide explained that the entire island was dependent on the pearl industry. Sam was amazed to learn that over four hundred thousand British pounds' worth of pearls (roughly two million US dollars' worth) were taken from the oyster beds each season. Now he realized why some of the local merchants were dressed in fine clothes and took extended trips to India.

The time passed quickly, and soon the steamer carrying Peter dropped anchor off Manamah. This was the moment Sam had looked forward to. Sam had not seen a family member since he said farewell to his father and brother Fred in Mainz, Germany, nearly two and a half years before.

Sam's reunion with his younger brother was a happy one. Peter was in fine health and eager to begin missionary work. As the two brothers journeyed on the steamer up the Persian Gulf to Basrah, Peter told Sam that their father was still fit and active. Although he was now nearly seventy years of age, Adriaan was a full-time pastor, with their sister Maud managing the house for him. There were now eight grandchildren, and their sister Mary was expecting another child any day. James, their oldest brother, had been elected president of Western Theological Seminary, while Fred was about to leave South Dakota to become a pastor in Graafschap, Michigan.

On hearing all the news, Sam felt a little homesick, but he knew he was blessed to now have his youngest brother at his side. Peter also reported that the missionary zeal at New Brunswick Theological Seminary seemed to be dwindling. He was the only member of his graduating class who had dedicated his life to mission work. But he also had some brighter missionary news. Dr. James Wyckoff, the son of a Reformed church pastor, had joined the Arabian Mission and would be arriving within the month. Sam's mind raced at the ways Dr. Wyckoff could help open doors for the gospel with his medical skills.

When the steamer docked at Basrah, Jim was waiting for Sam and Peter. The following day Sam and Jim showed Peter around the city, pointing out the many differences between Arab society and life back in the United States. Peter had a difficult time understanding that most women were kept in seclusion and some never left their houses. Sam cautioned his brother to never initiate a conversation with an Arab woman, but the caution was too much for Peter. "Jesus talked to the woman at the well!" he said. "Look at how our much our own sisters work to spread the gospel among men and women. This matter of the equality of the sexes is one of the glories of Christianity. Why should we not treat the women of Islam as we treat our own?"

Several days later Peter went for a walk. He returned to the house in a hurry, with men carrying sticks and stones chasing him. The mob slowly dispersed once Peter was safely in the house, and Peter recounted to Sam what had happened.

"I was walking by a graveyard, and I saw a lone woman weeping beside a grave. I walked up to her and tried to tell her that there is hope beyond the grave. She yelled that she was being accosted by a dog and an unbeliever and let out bloodcurdling screams. The men then arrived and started to chase me. It's a good thing I'm a fast runner," Peter added.

Sam smiled. His brother had learned an important lesson about life in Arabia the hard way, and he was grateful that no lasting harm had been done.

After several weeks the three missionaries got down to the business of deciding where they should start other permanent mission stations. It seemed a waste of resources for all three of them to remain in Basrah. As Jim and Sam had done upon Sam's arrival in Beirut, the men spread a map of Arabia out on the table. After praying over it, they all felt that God wanted Jim to stay in Basrah while Sam would open a new work in Bahrain. In the meantime, Peter would stay in Basrah for language study before going to start a new mission station. When Dr. Wyckoff arrived he would also stay in Basrah as he acclimatized to life in Arabia and then move to Bahrain to begin medical work there. Sam could hardly wait to have a medical doctor working alongside him. He still dreamed of opening a hospital in Arabia.

In February 1893, Sam set out for Bahrain. Before he left, Jim and Sam agreed that when Peter completed his language study in Basrah at the end of the year, he would go to Muscat on the Gulf of Oman and establish a new mission station. Sam was comforted to know that the two new mission stations would be only about five hundred miles apart, and he looked forward to being able to visit and support his younger brother.

Just as Sam expected, it proved difficult finding a place to rent in Manamah. But he persisted and eventually rented a twelve-by-twelve-foot room above the pearl market. The room had sixteen small windows without glass panes and a leaky roof.

The next challenge was to locate a place to set up a Bible shop. This involved a lot of haggling, but Sam won the day and rented a small store in the bazaar. The shop was located at the intersection of the street where the tinsmiths worked and sold their wares and where grocery items were sold.

The store space Sam rented was long and dark and open to the weather during the day. At night Sam secured the place by sliding upright boards into grooves and padlocking them together. Inside he set up a low bench covered with palm leaf matting. An upturned dry goods box served as a table, and a homemade bookcase housed Bibles and New Testaments along with other books in many languages. On the walls Sam hung a copy of the Lord's Prayer in Arabic, the English and Arabic alphabets, and a text telling all men everywhere to "repent, for the kingdom of heaven is at hand."

As he spent time at the Bible shop, Sam soon learned to distinguish the parade of characters who passed by: Arab pearl merchants who hurried along carrying large boxes; Persian men who sat down to chat and drink coffee with their countrymen; and an armorer who squatted all day opposite the shop, grinding swords, repairing flintlocks, and putting new handles on bowie knives. There were also Turkish soldiers returning footsore and hungry from the fighting on the Qatar Peninsula; chance pilgrims from India, who arrived on the various steamers that stopped in Bahrain; black slaves from Abyssinia; and closely veiled women navigating the street in silence.

Word spread quickly around Manamah that an American was selling Western books in the bazaar, and Sam quickly became adept at engaging local people in conversation. He would say, *"Ta'al shoof!* Come and see. Here is an Arabic gospel, a portion of the whole Injeel [New Testament] of Isa the prophet for only one anna. Have you read it? The Koran says it is 'light and guidance.' Or do you want to read the wonderful psalms of David in this pretty green binding for three annas? Here is the whole Torah [Old

Testament] in Persian for one rupee or a gilt-edged New Testament at two krans."

If a person disputed the authority of the Bible, Sam would reply, "You don't care to read the Holy Book because it has been corrupted, you say? How do you know if you have not read it? Do those on a caravan call the water bitter before they reach the well?" And if a person started to leave the shop, he would call after them, "Don't go away. I sell other books besides the Scriptures. Here is an atlas, all in Arabic; there are science primers, grammars, poetry, stories. Have you read *The Greatest Thing in the World* or *Swiss Family Robinson* put into Arabic?"

Hour after hour, day after day, Sam prayed and talked and tried to interest those who visited the Bible shop in the Old and New Testaments. He was pleased when someone would linger long enough to listen to a portion of the Bible.

While tending the Bible shop, Sam had plenty of time to watch the local "dentist" at work. The dentist was also the local blacksmith. He would drive small wooden wedges between the teeth to loosen an ulcerated or infected molar. He would then use his smithing pliers to extract the tooth. The procedure was bloody and painful, and Sam was convinced that he could do a better job. He sent to Bombay, India, for four dental forceps and a lancet. When the equipment arrived, he set up a dental clinic. He bought two red curtains and divided his room above the pearl market into three rooms. One room was his bedroom, the second a study, and the third room, closest to the door, was his dental surgery and dispensary. Wealthy people often preferred that Sam come to their homes to administer dental care, though this sometimes created problems, especially when a woman in the house had to be treated. In such cases Sam would find himself extracting troublesome teeth through a hole in a complete head veil.

Sam soon gained a reputation for "painless" dentistry, and it wasn't long before people started asking him for other types of medical aid. While Sam was not a trained doctor or dentist, he had taught himself enough of the basics of medical diagnosis and treatment and was glad to share what he knew with the residents of Manamah. Since no trained doctors or dentists were living in Bahrain, Sam often quoted an old Dutch proverb to himself: "In the land of the blind, the one-eyed man is king."

Now that he was involved in dispensing medicine, Sam waited eagerly for James Wyckoff to arrive. Instead, he received a depressing letter from Jim. Dr. Wyckoff, who had been in Arabia for only five months, had fallen ill with dysentery and relocated to the hill country of South India to recover. Jim wrote that he doubted the doctor would return anytime soon. This was a bitter blow for Sam and for the Arabian Mission. So far they'd had two doctors join them, and neither one had lasted more than six months. Despite his disappointment, Sam pressed on.

Within months of arriving, Sam felt like he was part of the fabric of Bahrain. He had sold 198 Scripture portions and 162 religious and educational books.

He saw other encouraging signs. One Muslim visitor bought a copy of the Gospel of John and slipped back later to confide in Sam that he believed that Jesus was the Son of God. Soon afterward a woman came in to buy a copy of the Psalms. Sam knew it was unwise to speak to her, but she whispered to him that she wanted to learn about the Jewish teachings and was able to read and write herself.

By the time Peter arrived in Muscat in November 1893, Sam felt that things were going well. His Arabic was improving, and he had made several loyal Muslim friends in Bahrain. There were also hints from the United States that big changes were on the horizon for the Arabian Mission.

Chapter 13

Miss Amy Elizabeth Wilkes

When Sam, Jim, and Philip Phelps—under the guidance of Dr. John Lansing—founded the Arabian Mission, they had hoped the organization would come under the umbrella of the mission board of the Reformed Church. At the time, the Reformed Church Mission Board had declined to take on the Arabian Mission because the mission board was severely in debt, with heavy financial commitments in India, China, and Japan.

Now, in 1894, circumstances had changed. The Arabian Mission was up and running and showing no signs of slowing down. The missionary letters Sam wrote and sent home were widely distributed by family and friends, who also brought their influence to bear on the Reformed Church Mission Board. As a result, in early 1894, Sam and Jim received a letter explaining that the mission board was willing to welcome the Arabian Mission into its fold and take over the administration and fund-raising responsibilities.

Sam and Jim were thrilled by the news. It took a load off their minds to know that a group of competent and experienced men back in the United States were willing to shoulder these responsibilities. They hoped there would now be a steady stream of qualified missionary recruits coming to work with them.

In the meantime, Sam kept busy with his work in Bahrain. By now it was obvious that Dr. Wyckoff would not be returning to Arabia. Despite his time of recuperation in the mountains of Southern India, the doctor could not rid himself of his illness and had decided to return to the United States. Sam administered health and dental care as best he could, praying always that another doctor would soon be appointed to work alongside him and take over the care of his patients.

With Peter now settled in Muscat, Sam received letters from his brother, filling him in on how the new mission station was progressing. The first house Peter had rented in Muscat was soon taken from him and turned over to the French consul to use as his residence. Peter had finally been able to secure another large house to rent. He had made a number of repairs to the place, but not to the roof. Peter's comical letter describing how the roof had caved in put a smile on Sam's face. Since no one was home at the time of the collapse, there were no casualties. Undeterred by these early housing setbacks, Peter persisted. He found another place to rent and managed to set up a Bible shop, where he sold portions of Scripture and other books to the locals. It was a promising start, and Peter persisted in improving his Arabic. Sam was proud of the job his brother was doing.

In March 1895, news of another one of Sam's brothers arrived in a letter from his father. This time it was not good news. Sam's thirty-four-year-old brother Adrian had died unexpectedly of pneumonia, leaving behind a widow, a two-month-old son, and his older son, John, from his first marriage. The news of Adrian's death saddened Sam and reminded him of how life could quickly be taken away, even in a place like America with modern medical facilities.

At the end of March, Sam found himself in Basrah, visiting Jim, who had been serving the mission in Arabia for five-and-a-half years. Jim was planning to return to the United States for furlough, and Sam wanted to spend some time with him before he departed. The two young men were busy praying together and strategizing about future mission stations when a telegraph arrived. Jim read it and quickly handed it over for Sam to read. "Miss Alice Philips and Miss Amy Elizabeth Wilkes arriving Basrah SS *Clan Cameron*, April 1, five p.m. Please meet and see on to Baghdad. Much obliged CMS."

Jim and Sam looked at each other and then sprang into action. The young women would be arriving the following day, and Jim's house was a mess. The men needed to make the place look more homelike. Sam laughed as he swept and dusted and watched Jim shove a pile of books and boxes under a table and then cover the whole thing with a long tablecloth. The following morning Sam washed and dried two new china cups he'd just bought at the market and eagerly awaited the time of the arrival of the steamer in Basrah. He and Jim were about to meet and entertain two young Christian women—something neither of them had done in years!

Sam and Jim were waiting on the dock when the SS *Clan Cameron* arrived on time. They watched as two very attractive young women disembarked. They introduced themselves to the two women, who told them that they were from Sydney, Australia. Amy Wilkes, a tall brunette, informed Sam that she was a nurse who had been born in England and then moved to Australia.

Sam and Jim collected the women's baggage and arranged for it to be transported to Jim's house while they escorted the new arrivals there.

Back at Jim's house, Sam and Jim made a pot of tea, and Sam arranged the new teacups on the table. He then walked over and peered out the window while Amy poured the tea. "Look, there's a caravan passing by," he exclaimed.

As Amy ran to the window to catch her first glimpse of an Arabian caravan, her foot caught the edge of the tablecloth, pulling it, along with the teapot and china cups and saucers, off the edge of the table. With a loud crash, everything hit the floor and shattered.

At the sight of what she had done, Amy rushed out onto the balcony and burst into tears. Sam and Jim looked at each other, not sure what to do. Finally Sam ventured out to comfort Amy. "Don't worry," he said, trying to think of something funny to say. "They are only things. You can come back here anytime you like and break every dish in the house. No one would really care, you know."

Amy smiled weakly and dabbed her brown eyes with her handkerchief. "I'm not normally like this," she said. "I don't cry at everything; I'm just very tired. It's been quite the trip getting this far."

Sam nodded. He knew exactly what she meant. Adjusting to the heat, the smells, and the strange customs on top of all the travel could be overwhelming. "Jim and I will do whatever we can to help you," he said, and he meant it. In fact, Sam volunteered to accompany the two CMS novice missionaries to Baghdad. They arrived there just in time for Sam's twenty-eighth birthday on April 12.

Sam returned to Bahrain, but he soon found an excuse to return to Baghdad, where he offered to help Amy with her language learning. Over the next few months, Sam made numerous trips to Baghdad, spending more time there than in Bahrain. The truth was, Sam had fallen in love with Amy, and before long he asked her to marry him. She accepted his proposal and on May 18, 1896, a little more than a year after they met, Samuel Marinus Zwemer and Amy Elizabeth Wilkes were married at the British consulate in Baghdad.

Their marriage meant that Amy needed to switch from being a CMS missionary to a missionary with the Arabian Mission. Since she had not completed her three-year commitment to the CMS, she was required to repay part of the cost of her passage to Arabia from Australia. Sam paid the money and often joked that he'd had to buy his wife in true Middle Eastern style!

Just a week after their wedding, Sam received an astonishing letter from his brother Peter. Peter had assumed the legal responsibility for eighteen African boys aged seven to thirteen years. When they heard the news, Sam and Amy took a steamer to Muscat to learn the whole story and see how they could help out.

When they arrived at the mission house in Muscat, Sam found his brother surrounded by eighteen dark faces from East Africa. Each boy had an identical burn mark on his left cheek. "How on earth did you come to have custody of these boys?" Sam asked.

"It's a simple story really," Peter began. "You know well enough what a problem slavery is in this part of the world, and how the British are trying to put a stop to it. A Royal Navy frigate, the HMS *Lapwig*, captured two Arab slave *dhows* off the coast of Oman. These eighteen boys from East Africa, all on their way to be sold as slaves, were on the boat. All the boys have been branded, as you can see. The British ship brought them here to Muscat. Because no one knew what port the boys had come from in East Africa, they could not be returned home. Instead, they were released into the custody of the British consul here. Of course, this wasn't a very satisfactory arrangement. The boys are all aged thirteen and under, and they ran up and down the verandas of the consulate. They got into everything and made quite a nuisance of themselves. The consul was in despair. He didn't quite know what to do with them. That's when I decided to step in. I talked to the consul and offered to take the boys. I must say, he was more than a little eager to hand custody over to me," Peter added with a chuckle.

"But what do you propose to do with the boys?" Sam asked.

"The Freed Slaves School," Peter answered. "All of the boys speak only Swahili. At the school we give them lessons in Arabic and English as well as arithmetic, other practical subjects, and, of course, Bible study. With the knowledge the boys gain, they'll be able to be employed and earn a living and make their own way in the world. Why, some of them might even become missionaries."

Peter went on to explain that he expected the school to grow. With the British determined to stamp out the slave trade between East Africa and Arabia, it was only a matter of time before more children on their way to a life of slavery would be intercepted by British ships and brought to the school.

Sam was touched by his brother's zeal to see that the boys had the necessary skills to make their own way in life. He also chuckled when Peter explained that he had given the boys English names. He began by naming them after members of his own family, with his favorite being named Adrian, after their father and deceased brother. The biggest of the boys he named James, after their oldest brother.

Once Sam felt his brother had the Freed Slaves School on a steady footing, he and Amy set off for Bahrain. Sam was excited to show his bride her new home, but he was a little concerned too. He knew many things could go wrong for a missionary couple, especially when they were the only two Christians in an entire country.

Amy seemed to like Bahrain and set to work bringing a woman's touch to the house she and Sam rented. She soon found herself as busy as her husband. In Bahrain, as in the other Muslim countries Sam had visited, men and women seldom mixed. There were strict religious laws about their not being alone together and not touching each other for any reason. Before long, women were seeking Amy out to help them with their medical concerns. As a nurse, Amy was glad to help, and she soon joined Sam in his dream of establishing a hospital.

In fall of 1896, Jim returned from furlough and took up his mission responsibilities in Basrah. In early 1897, less than a year after they were married, Sam and Amy went on furlough to the United States. By now Sam had been in Arabia for seven years, and he was eager to introduce his new wife to his family. Not only that, but Amy was also pregnant with their first child, who would be born while they were in the United States. Before he set out for home, Sam left a colporteur to take charge of the Bible shop.

Sam loved the trip back by steamer. He and Amy stopped at Aden, and Sam showed Amy where he and Jim had lived in Crater Town. As they steamed up the Red Sea, he pointed out the various places he had visited. When the steamer dropped anchor off Al Hudaydah, Sam told Amy about setting out from this city on his trip inland and the amazing things he had seen in Sana'a. Chugging up the Red Sea in the steamer, Sam thought about his trip down to Aden to join Jim over six years earlier. Then, he had known little about Arabia and the people who lived there. Now he knew so much more, and was a better missionary as a result.

When the couple arrived in the United States, Sam enjoyed many reunions with old friends and colleagues. He stopped at the New Brunswick Seminary to speak to the student body before heading to Michigan to reunite with his father and siblings. He had hoped to see Dr. Lansing, but John was no longer teaching at the seminary. He had retired because of his poor health and had moved to Denver, Colorado.

Sam and Amy made it to Spring Lake, Michigan, about twenty miles north of Holland, where his father was now living. Adriaan welcomed his son home and enjoyed getting to know his new daughter-in-law. Sam's sister Maud still lived with their father, keeping house for him and assisting him in his ministry. Over the next few weeks, a procession of Sam's other siblings visited him to catch up on all that had happened during Sam's time in Arabia. Their visits gave Sam a chance to hold his new nieces and nephews for the first time. It was a sad occasion when Sam visited the grave of his brother Adrian.

On May 23, 1897, while still in Spring Lake, Michigan, Amy gave birth to a daughter, whom they named Katharine, after Sam's mother. As far as Sam was concerned, Katharine was the most beautiful baby in the world, and he was a proud father.

Several weeks after the birth of Katharine, Sam left Amy and the baby with his father and sister and set out on a strenuous round of speaking engagements. When he had departed for Arabia, the Arabian Mission had been an independent mission. Now that it was part of the Reformed Church's missionary network, Sam had many obligations to fulfill.

Wherever he went, Sam spoke about the needs and challenges of the Arabian mission stations. He spoke about the Freed Slaves School his brother had started in Muscat and how the school needed sponsors. Most importantly, Sam spoke of the need for doctors to establish a hospital in Bahrain.

Sam's speaking began to pay off. Dr. Fred Barny soon volunteered to work with the Arabian Mission and was quickly dispatched to Basrah. Sam hoped that this doctor would be with the mission longer than the first two who had come to serve.

Sam met with Margaret Rice, who was engaged to marry Fred, and arranged for her to sail to Arabia with him and Amy when they returned from furlough and to marry Fred. Sam also met with George Stone, a Presbyterian minister who had heard of the Arabian Mission through his involvement in the

Student Volunteer Movement. George explained to Sam that he had tried every possible way to avoid going to the foreign mission field, but he could not find peace until he applied to serve with the Arabian Mission.

Sam liked George immediately and arranged for him also to travel back with him and Amy at the end of their furlough. There was also more good news. Sam talked with Sharon Thoms and his wife, Marion, who were both doctors, committed Christians, and graduates of the University of Michigan Medical School. They asked many questions regarding the mission and were excited about being a part of the new medical work in Bahrain.

In early 1898, Sam received some discouraging news. His brother Peter had taken ill in Muscat. Peter was so ill that he was returning to the United States for medical care. Sam began to fret about his brother's well-being. Jim, who had gone to Muscat to carry on the mission work during Peter's illness, had written Sam that Peter had been so weak he was carried aboard the steamer on a stretcher for the voyage home.

When Peter arrived in New York City on July 12, 1898, he was taken straight from the ship to Presbyterian Hospital. Sam went to New York to visit his brother. He found Peter lying in a hospital bed, weak and pale but totally engaged in the mission work in Muscat. Peter explained to Sam that he was writing a report to the mission board outlining the changes he thought were necessary for the mission house in

Muscat to make it more suitable for their work. Peter also talked about the Freed Slaves School and gave Sam a report on how the boys were doing. "I tell you, I've done nothing yet. When I go back to Arabia, I'll be ready to begin work," Peter told Sam. As he listened to his brother talk, Sam smiled at Peter's zeal and enthusiasm for mission work throughout Arabia. He just hoped that Peter would make a quick and full recovery. At the end of his visit, Sam said farewell to his brother, and the two of them promised to get together as soon as Peter returned to Muscat.

Shortly before Sam set sail to return to Arabia on August 17, 1898, he received a letter from Sharon and Marion Thoms saying that they were volunteering to serve with the Arabian Mission and hoped to join him the following year.

Sam, Amy, and baby Katharine, accompanied by Margaret Rice and George Stone, set sail from New York City aboard the steamer *Majestic*, bound for Liverpool, England. From there they would travel to Egypt and then sail through the Suez Canal, down the Red Sea, and around the south coast of the Arabian Peninsula to Karachi, Pakistan, where they would catch another steamer for the last leg of the journey. They were all ready and eager to embrace the mission work that lay ahead of them.

Chapter 14

A Hospital at Last

At the beginning of October 1898, the band of missionaries arrived in Karachi, Pakistan, to change ships for the trip to Bahrain. Dr. Fred Barny was waiting for them or, more importantly, for his fiancée, Margaret Rice. Fred had spent time in both Basrah and Muscat and had come to Karachi to get married. While the Zwemers and George Stone traveled on to Bahrain, Fred and Margaret were married in Karachi. Following their honeymoon, they traveled to Muscat to assist Jim with the mission work there.

Soon after arriving back in Bahrain, Sam received a telegram from the United States. His brother Peter had died on October 18. Peter's body was being taken back to Michigan so that he could be buried beside their mother and brother Adrian. It was a bitter blow to Sam. When he had left Peter's side in the hospital, he was sure he would see him again.

As he grieved over his brother's death, Sam reread the missionary newsletters Peter had sent out and found comfort in them. In one of them Peter had written, "No government or priest can forbid the simple conversing with friends concerning religion, and when they, inadvertently perhaps, purchase the Scriptures, we may put to them the question of Philip to the eunuch of Candace: 'Understandest thou what thou readest?' In this sense all Muslim lands are accessible, and in this way we are privileged to witness the truth as it is in Jesus to many."

Sam took heart in Peter's message and legacy. While it was difficult and often illegal to reach the Muslim population en masse, it *was* possible to quietly go about doing good and having conversations with individuals about Jesus Christ. An incident that occurred the following week reinforced this. An old Arab man visited Sam. He understood a lot about Christianity and asked for a Bible to read. He returned often to talk and ask questions about the Bible. As he came day after day, Sam noticed that he always had an old bandage wrapped around his foot. Finally Sam asked the old man what was wrong with his foot. "Oh, that old bandage is just an excuse for those who ask why I come to see you so often. The foot is all right." Sam chuckled at the old man's inventiveness. In such private conversations, the work of sharing the gospel continued.

In Bahrain, Sam and Amy committed to stay on the island and expand the mission station there until their next furlough. There was a lot they wanted to accomplish before then. One thing Sam wanted to do was to write a book. He felt this was the best way to convey information about the Muslim world and inspire new missionary recruits to work in Arabia. Sam began writing a book titled *Arabia: The Cradle of Islam: Studies in the Geography, People and Politics of the Peninsula with an Account of Islam and Mission Work.* Writing a book was a challenge, but one Sam enjoyed.

While Sam labored away in Bahrain, Jim worked in Muscat and oversaw the Freed Slaves School. George went to Basrah to acclimatize to life in Arabia and to learn the language. George was soon joined by the Thomses when they arrived from the United States.

Following his time in Basrah, George went to Muscat to work with Jim. Sadly, within ten months of arriving in Arabia, George fell ill. Jim sent him to convalesce a few miles up the coast in Birka, where the heat was not so intense. On June 28, 1899, George wrote from Birka to say that he was feeling better. Within hours of writing and sending the letter, he suffered severe heatstroke and died. His body was wrapped in an old sail and returned to the dock at Muscat, where Jim was asked to claim it. George was buried next to the grave of Thomas Valpy French in Cemetery Cove at Muscat.

When news of George's death reached him in Bahrain, Sam was stunned. He wondered what it could mean. His brother Peter and George Stone, the two youngest and physically strongest of the members of the Arabian Mission, had fallen ill and died within nine months of each other. Sam wrote another missionary newsletter home, addressing the deaths.

> If the death of two American missionaries for Muscat does not awaken men to the needs of dark Eastern Arabia, what will? Being dead, our brothers will speak. You know what their message would be if they spoke it from your pulpit or in your parlor. It would be a message like that of [Johann Ludwig] Krapf [a German missionary, explorer, and linguist] from East Africa: "Our God bids us first build a cemetery before we build a church or dwelling house, showing that the resurrection of East Africa must be effected by our own destruction. Our sanguine expectations and hopes of immediate success may be laid in the grave like Lazarus, yet they shall have a resurrection and our eyes shall see the glory of the Lord at last."

Despite the setback from the deaths, the missionaries had some breakthroughs. On Saturday, June 30, 1899, the first baptisms took place in Bahrain. Lydia and her three children, Nejma, Razouki, and Mejid, had fled to Bahrain from Baghdad to escape being forcibly kept in the Muslim religion. The Turkish authorities there had threatened to force Lydia to marry a Muslim and put her children into a Turkish government school. Amazingly, Lydia and her children were able to sneak out of Baghdad, make their way to Bahrain and the mission station, and receive more instruction in the Christian faith. Lydia and her children professed their desire to be baptized. The Sunday afternoon following the baptism, Lydia met with Sam and Amy and about twelve other people for a church service, where she received her first communion.

Also in 1899, in Bahrain, Amy gave birth to another daughter. She and Sam named the new baby Nellie Elizabeth Zwemer, though everyone called her Bessie.

At the beginning of December 1899, the Reverend Harry J. Wiersum arrived from the United States to serve with the mission. Like most new recruits, he went to Basrah to acclimatize to the Arabian living conditions. He began learning the language, which he noted in a letter to Sam as "a most difficult and perplexing language."

Sam tried hard to keep his friends and supporters at home informed about what he was up to, but it was hard to describe just how different life was in Bahrain. On the evening of December 7, 1899, he sat down to write a New Year's newsletter home. Sam spent much of the letter describing what a normal day was like for him in Bahrain.

Today it was a bright, cool day of our mild winter. At this season the weather does not hinder mission work nor melt enthusiasm. We rose at about six o'clock, and while Mrs. Zwemer was dressing the children, I read to her from John's Epistle. Our reading was interrupted by an early caller, a *Banian* (Hindu) merchant, who came to purchase a map of

Bahrain and an atlas he could not find at the bookshop the day before. He remained for some time and took other books with him, but as some of them were on Christianity, he politely returned them afterward. Our breakfast was next in order, and then the household, including our colporteurs, met in the study for morning prayer. We read Psalm 31 by turns and, after brief comments, Jusef [a colporteur] led in prayer. Already a dozen or more patients were at the doorway waiting for the dispensary to open.

Sam went on to describe how after their morning prayer time Jusef was sent with books to the weekly bazaar held on Thursdays at Suk-el-Khamis, about two miles away. Sam and a helper, Gibrail, tended to the patients awaiting medical care. Sam described treating patients with fever, ulcers, eye infections, and dysentery. Amy came later in the morning to tend to Muslim women and children.

Between treating patients, Sam and Gibrail managed to sell eight copies of the Gospel of John. Sam even noted what he ate for lunch—mutton, eggplant, rice, native bread, and pudding. Following afternoon prayers, Sam tended to more patients while Amy went out on an afternoon excursion. She took bundles of infant clothes made by Reformed Church women in the United States and distributed them to needy children. Along the way, Amy was invited into a house where she spoke with ten women about the Third Commandment—not taking the Lord's name in vain—and answered all sorts of questions the women asked about the Christian way of living and worship.

After seeing patients and tending to a few other small matters, Sam managed to get a little time to read before eating dinner and putting the children to bed. But his day was not yet done. In the evening he delivered a talk in English and Arabic to a number of local merchants about his travels, illustrating the talk with magic lantern slides projected onto a white sheet hung for the purpose. In everything Sam did, he sought to give a practical demonstration of God's love and compassion for people and to search out those moments of private conversation where he could share the gospel directly. Sam finished his rendition of the day's activities by writing, "The day is done. Such is a glimpse of our daily round and common task."

As 1899 drew to a close, Sam completed work on his book on Arabia and sent the manuscript to a publisher in New York City. As the New Year rolled around, Sam kept busy with his mission work in Bahrain. He was thrilled when *Arabia: The Cradle of Islam: Studies in the Geography, People and Politics of the Peninsula with an Account of Islam and Mission Work* was published in the first half of the year and received many good reviews. Sam was even happier when, later in 1900, he received news from Dr. Alfred DeWitt Mason, a former treasurer of the Arabian Mission. Dr. DeWitt and his brother in Brooklyn, New York, were donating six thousand dollars from their father's estate to build a hospital in Bahrain. For Sam it was a dream come true. Not only did he now have two doctors working alongside him in Bahrain (Sharon and Marion Thoms had moved to the island after their time in Basrah), but he also had the money to start moving ahead with the hospital he'd dreamed about for so long. Sam was glad to have the Thomses in Bahrain to assist Amy with the birth of her third healthy daughter, whom they named Ruth. Sam was delighted to be a father again.

As Sam moved ahead with the hospital, he soon discovered that it would be the start of two years of constant frustrations and negotiations. It had been difficult when Sam first came to Bahrain to find a landlord willing to rent a house to Christian missionaries. The same proved true in finding a suitable plot of land on which to build a hospital. Even though the local residents of Manamah acknowledged the value of medical care, no one was willing to sell the mission a plot of land. The rich were content with American doctors treating them in their own homes, and they did not see a need to give poor people medical attention. Sam visited Sheikh Isa bin Ali, the ruler of Bahrain, and asked him if he would sell the mission a plot of land he owned on the outskirts of Manamah. The sheikh received Sam warmly, but when Sam asked about the land, the sheikh's advisers had all kinds of objections and reasons why such a sale could never take place.

Sam was frustrated and disappointed. Then he learned of another plot of land for sale. Sam quickly reached an agreement with the owner. He signed a bill of sale and paid a deposit of half the purchase price. He was elated as he made his way home to tell Amy and the Thomses of the purchase.

Sam's elation was short-lived, however. Later that night Hassan Musherif, a Muslim friend of Sam's, arrived at the mission house dressed in a disguise. He apologized for coming so late and explained that the disguise was so that no one would recognize him. "You have been deceived," he told Sam. "You must take back the bill of sale for the land and get back your money."

Sam was surprised by the unexpected turn of events.

"They have played a trick on you," Hassan said. "The land you have been sold is the site of an old ruined mosque. Once you start building, the authorities will declare the property *wag* (sacred) and stop your work. You will lose everything."

The next morning Sam went to talk to the owner of the plot. Without betraying Hassan's confidence, he confronted the owner over the deceit and left with his deposit back and the bill of sale torn up. Sam was glad to have his money back, but he was no closer to securing land.

For the next month Sam and Amy and the other missionaries serving with them in Bahrain prayed and waited. Just when it seemed that they had reached a dead end in the search for a suitable hospital building site, Sam received some astonishing news. A trusted adviser to Sheikh Isa bin Ali had

had a dream in which he saw *Nebi Isa* (Jesus). In the dream Jesus had told him to sell a parcel of land to the missionaries. As a result of the dream, the sheikh wanted to reopen negotiations with Sam. On August 16, 1901, an agreement was reached with the sheikh to purchase the land for four thousand rupees.

With the purchase of the land complete, plans were quickly drawn up for a two-story building surrounded on three sides by twelve-foot-wide verandas. The structure would be built of limestone that was brought to the building site from the shores of the island. Stonemasons were hired to set the stone, while carpenters made doors and windows from teak imported from Bombay, India. The hinges and locks for the doors and windows, along with all the paint and varnish used, were imported from London.

With Sharon and Marion Thoms treating the patients who flocked to the mission each day for medical care, Sam was now free to oversee the construction of the hospital. But he faced many challenges along the way. For one, in this part of Arabia it was customary for a blood sacrifice to be made at the four corners of the foundation to ward off accidents on the building site. Without such a sacrifice, the builders would not work on the building. The animals were slaughtered, as was customary, and Sam put on a large barbecue for the builders.

Work on the project during the blazing heat of summer was slow. When winter arrived and Sam hoped to gain speed on the project, cholera broke out on the island, causing more delays. Problems with the design of the staircases and the roof had to be solved before work could proceed again. Besides all this, the stonemasons and carpenters needed constant supervision. Sam learned that if left unsupervised, workers would stop, stand around, and talk and smoke. The workers also had to be continually coaxed to do quality work. Otherwise, they would take shortcuts and produce inferior work that often had to be redone, wasting time and materials.

Sam was so focused on the new hospital that he sometimes lost sight of what was going on at the other Arabian Mission stations. Additional volunteers had arrived from the United States to serve with the mission. As the hospital building was taking shape, Sam learned that one of the volunteers, Harry J. Wiersum, had died on August 3, 1901. Harry had been serving at the mission station in Basrah, where he had contracted smallpox. He was the third strong, young missionary recruit to die while serving with the mission in Arabia.

During 1901, with the building of the hospital continuing, Sam took on a new challenge—writing another book, this time a biography of Raymund Lull, who was considered to be the first missionary to Muslims. Raymund was born in 1235 in the city of Palma on the island of Majorca. He came from a wealthy and distinguished family and was a brilliant man in his time. As a result, he became a courtier to King James II of Aragon and was also the court poet. Although he was married and had several young children, Raymund tried to woo the wife of another court official. But while composing a suggestive poem to this woman, he had a vision of Christ hanging on the cross and looking at him with shame. As a result of this experience, at the age of twenty-eight, Raymund fell under conviction of his sin and became a vibrant Christian.

Following his conversion, Raymund felt a burden to reach Muslims with the gospel. He spent nine years studying the Arabic language and Muslim culture, philosophy, and religion. After mastering the Muslim language and culture, he challenged others to go as missionaries to Muslims. When no one took up the challenge, he decided to go himself. He traveled several times to Tunisia in North Africa, where he openly debated Muslim scholars, a number of whom eventually professed faith in Jesus Christ. His actions did not go unnoticed. On his third trip to North Africa at age eighty-two, Raymund was stoned by a crowd of angry Muslims in the city of Bougie. A Genoese merchant took the injured Raymund back to Palma, where he died the following year.

As he studied Raymund Lull's story, Sam found the man inspiring. As he began to write the biography, in the preface he noted:

> There is no more heroic figure in the history of Christendom than that of Raymund Lull, the first and perhaps the greatest missionary to Mohammedans. No complete biography of Lull exists in the English language; and . . . we should rescue the memory of [this] pioneer

from oblivion. . . . His self-sacrificing love
never faileth and its memory cannot perish.
His biography emphasizes his own motto: *"He
who lives by the Life cannot die."* It is this part of
Lull's life that has a message for us today and
calls us to win back the Mohammedan world
to Christ.

While Sam studied and wrote the biography of
Raymund Lull, he kept busy supervising the building
of the hospital. Despite his many responsibilities, Sam
made good progress on the biography and completed
it in early 1902. It was a happy day on the morning
of March 30, 1902, when Sam wrapped up the manuscript and mailed it to his publisher in England. It
was an even happier day for him that afternoon when
Amy gave birth to another child, this time a son. In
honor of the just-completed biography, Sam and Amy
named their new son Raymund Lull Zwemer. They
prayed that he would be a great missionary in Arabia,
just like his namesake. Now the Zwemers had four
children: Katharine, Bessie, Ruth, and Raymund.

Throughout 1902 work progressed on the building of the hospital. Since the new facility would need
an adequate supply of fresh water, the workers dug a
well on the property. However, the water they found
was brackish and unusable. But the arrival of a windmill from a church in Waupun, Wisconsin, changed
the equation. They would be able to dig the well
much deeper, find good water, and use the windmill
to pump the water to the surface.

The windmill arrived in Bahrain in pieces, accompanied by two wrenches and a set of instructions on how to put it together. The tower of the windmill was assembled on its side on the ground. A wooden tank was put in place to hold the water after it was pumped to the surface. Everything was ready to hoist the windmill into place. That was when the trouble began. A crowd of several hundred people gathered to see the windmill being hoisted by a group of men using ropes and a pulley. But when the tower of the windmill got halfway up, it buckled and fell back to the ground, where it lay in a twisted heap. As he viewed the wrecked windmill, Sam cried from disappointment and despair. That night he wondered whether the hospital would ever be finished.

The next morning the SS *Assyria*, a steamer that regularly plied the Persian Gulf, stopped at Bahrain. Over the course of the many stops the steamer had made in Bahrain, Sam had become friends with the vessel's engineer. Sam visited the man at the ship and told him about the wrecked windmill. The engineer laughed when he saw the twisted heap of metal. He told Sam that their mistake had been in putting too much strain on the tower as they hoisted it up. Before long a group of sailors arrived from the ship and set to work on the windmill. They brought a portable forge with them and began straightening the bent angle irons and strengthening the tower. Then, under the watchful eye of the ship's engineer, they hoisted the windmill into place. Sam was thrilled, and before long the windmill was pumping water.

More blunders were made installing the water pipes, which carried water to the operating room washbasins and the women's ward. The pipes leaked badly the first time water flowed through them. But the problem was soon discovered, and the pipes were refitted, this time with white lead in the joints. To Sam's relief, there were no more leaks.

As December 1902 arrived, the new hospital building was nearing completion. Sam left Sharon Thoms in charge of overseeing the finishing touches to the building while he headed to India. Sam had been invited to attend the Fourth Decennial Indian Missionary Conference that was to be held in Madras from December 11 to December 18. He hoped that by the time he returned from the conference, everything would be in order with the new building. He was anxious to see the hospital dedicated and put to use ministering to the medical needs of the residents of Bahrain.

Chapter 15

The Cost of Success

Sam arrived in Madras, on the southeastern coast of India, just in time for the start of the Fourth Decennial Indian Missionary Conference. The interdenominational conference was held once every ten years. About two hundred missionaries were attending from all over India and Burma, and since Sam served in Arabia, he was glad to be invited.

The conference reminded Sam of his days in the Student Volunteer Movement back in the United States, organizing and speaking at events in churches and on college and seminary campuses. Just as in those days, it seemed to Sam that everyone attending this conference had interesting and challenging stories to tell. In fact, the atmosphere of the conference

167

energized him. After so many months of focusing on the building of the hospital in Bahrain, it felt good to be reminded of the larger, worldwide missionary challenge that faced the Christian church.

As Sam listened to missionaries from different denominations and missions speak, he realized that many of the struggles he and his team faced in Bahrain were similar to those faced by missionaries working among India's Muslim population. There were the issues of ministering to women who were mostly hidden from view, the difficulty in sharing the gospel openly, and the passive and sometimes active opposition that developed in Muslim communities, making life difficult for missionaries.

As the conference progressed, Sam noticed something else. Although a fifth of the population of India was Muslim, missionary work among them did not feature largely on the conference agenda. When Sam asked other missionaries why this was, they told him that working among Muslims was discouraging and few people understood the particular problems Muslim evangelism presented. Their answer gave Sam an idea: Why not hold a missionary conference especially for those missionaries working among Muslims, regardless of the country they were in? Sam talked to several of the conference attendees about the idea and received an enthusiastic response from them. He set to work organizing a first-of-its-kind conference that would be invaluable to the many discouraged missionaries working among Muslim populations.

Energized and excited, Sam headed straight back to Bahrain after the conference in Madras. He was pleased when he arrived to find that the new hospital building was finished. For him, it was a beautiful sight to behold, and one for which he was very grateful.

In January 1903, the annual meeting of the Arabian Mission was held in Bahrain. This was a time when all the Arabian Mission missionaries serving at the various mission stations throughout the region gathered for fellowship, prayer, and strategizing. On Sunday, January 26, the missionaries attended the dedication service of the new Mason Memorial Hospital. During the service Sam gave an address, and then Jim offered a prayer of dedication for the new facility.

As Jim dedicated the hospital to God and to the people of Arabia, Sam fought back tears. After so many struggles and so many answers to prayer, the hospital—his dream, and the only hospital of its kind in Arabia—was complete and ready to receive its first patients. After the formal dedication, Sam joined in the singing of a new hymn written for the occasion. "Accept this building, gracious Lord, / No temple though it be; / We raise it for our suffering poor / And so, good Lord, for Thee."

Soon the new hospital was filled with activity. Not only were more patients than ever coming for treatment, but new workers were arriving to help. Elizabeth DePree, a nurse and the first single woman recruit in the Arabian Mission, worked alongside

Doctors Sharon and Marion Thoms, busily treating patients. James Moerdyk from Drenthe, Michigan, who had a gift for business administration, helped with hospital management. Later Jane Scardefield arrived to help with the mission's outreach in Bahrain, particularly among the women and children.

With things at the new hospital running fairly smoothly, Sam turned his attention back to organizing the conference for missionaries working among Muslim populations. He corresponded with Dr. H. U. Weitbracht of the Church Missionary Society in Lahore, India, whom he had met at the conference in Madras. As the two corresponded, the outline of the new conference came into focus. It would be held in Cairo, Egypt, between April 4 and 9, 1906, and Sam would serve as the chairman of the organizing committee. A number of smaller committees were formed to oversee various aspects of the conference agenda and make sure that as many missionaries as possible were invited.

With the active planning under way for the Cairo Conference, as it was being called, Sam set out to write a book on the Muslim view of the character of God as seen through the Koran and Muslim tradition. He titled the book *The Moslem Doctrine of God*, which he hoped to have published in time for the conference in Cairo.

In late August 1903, as Sam was working out more details of the planned Cairo Conference, word reached him that his brother Fred had died following a short illness. The news seemed almost unbelievable.

When Sam had last seen him, Fred was healthy and fit, and now he was dead. Sam wished he could be at the funeral, but he knew that was impossible. He prayed for Fred's wife and children and wrote letters to comfort them in their loss.

More family deaths, ones that were much closer to home, were to follow. In June 1904 as Sam managed the work of the mission in Bahrain, worked on planning the Cairo Conference, and wrote chapter after chapter of his new book, a typhoid epidemic swept through the island. Many of the residents of Bahrain died as a result, but the Zwemer family remained healthy. But just when the danger from the epidemic seemed to have passed, two of Sam's daughters, seven-year-old Katharine and four-year-old Ruth, fell ill with a fever. Despite the best medical care the hospital could offer, it was not enough. On July 7, 1904, Ruth died. A week later Katharine also died. Before her death, Katharine had asked her parents to sing her favorite hymn, "Thou Art Coming, O My Savior," for her. Together Sam and Amy sang:

> Thou art coming, O, my Saviour!
> Thou art coming, O, my King!
> In Thy beauty all-resplendent,
> In Thy glory all-transcendent;
> Well may we rejoice and sing!
> Coming! in the opening east,
> Herald brightness slowly swells!
> Coming! O, my glorious Priest,
> Hear we not Thy golden bells?

The death of their two daughters was a punishing blow to Sam and Amy. Their beautiful girls were gone. The two girls were buried in the same grave and on the headstone were inscribed the words, "Worthy is the Lamb that was slain to receive riches."

Following the deaths of Katharine and Ruth, Sam found it difficult to continue his work without the sound of the girls' laughter in the air. Sometimes he was overcome with deep sadness. At other times their memory spurred him on to work even harder to save the lives of the other young children who came to the hospital for treatment.

In March 1905, eight months after the deaths of Ruth and Katharine, Sam and Amy and their two surviving children, Bessie and Raymund, set off for furlough. As they sailed back to the United States, Sam realized that more than six years had passed since their previous furlough. So much had happened in that time. The Arabian Mission had grown, with sixteen missionaries now serving at three mission station and plans in the works to open a new mission station in Kuwait. Not only that, the Mason Memorial Hospital was now open and ministering to the medical needs of the residents of Bahrain and beyond.

All this success had come at a cost, and for the Zwemers that cost had been the deaths of Ruth and Katharine. But even after that tragedy, God had been faithful, and Amy was pregnant once again. Another child would be born while they were on furlough. Then there was the upcoming Cairo Conference the following year. Sam was certain this would be a turning point in outreach and missionary work among Muslim people.

When they reached the United States, Sam and Amy headed to Michigan to stay with Sam's father and sister. Several weeks after arriving home, Sam got word in Michigan that Dr. Marion Thoms had died on April 25, 1905. She and her husband had been running the hospital in Bahrain. Marion's death deeply saddened both Sam and Amy. During the years they had worked together in Bahrain, the Thomses had become good friends as well as faithful coworkers. Sam and Amy wrote a tribute to Marion which was published in the Arabian Mission newsletter.

> She was not merely a missionary's wife, but herself a heroic and strong and self-denying missionary. Her triumphant deathbed showed that her thoughts even then were not only for her own, but for dark Arabia. Among her last words was the message: 'Have them send more missionaries for the work and to take the place of those [who] fall by the way.' Everyone who knew Mrs. Thoms will remember her thorough conscientiousness and her heroic devotion. She was often ready at the call of duty and often, alas, worked above her strength for her Arabian sisters. They knew it, and loved her. Her skill and patience as a physician, her faithfulness in language study, her self-effacement and humility, her power in prayer for others, and her cheerfulness—they all come up before us as we read of her death.

The good news was that another doctor, Arthur Bennett, along with his wife, was now stationed at the hospital in Bahrain. He was able to assist Sharon Thoms as he carried on the medical care at the hospital.

Sam and Amy also received more good news from Arabia. On September 22, 1905, Jim Cantine and Elizabeth DePree were married in Landour, India. Following the couple's return to Arabia, Elizabeth moved from Bahrain to Muscat, where Jim was still overseeing the mission station and running the Freed Slaves School.

Amy gave birth to another child in Michigan, a daughter whom she and Sam named Amy Ruth Zwemer, after her mother and deceased sister.

Throughout 1905 Sam kept busy traveling and speaking in churches around the United States. He was seeking to raise money to support the ongoing work of the Arabian Mission and challenging people with the need for more missionaries to win Muslims to Christ. While he was doing all this, Sam organized the Cairo Conference for the following year. He was arranging for a number of prominent missionaries to write papers on various issues related to mission work among Muslims. The papers would then be presented at the conference. Sam had almost completed *The Moslem Doctrine of God*, still hoping it would be published by the time the conference started.

In March 1906, a year after going on furlough to the United States, Sam set out for Egypt and the Cairo Conference. The conference was held in a large, stately house in the center of Cairo. At the opening of the conference, sixty-two delegates were representing twenty-nine different mission societies. Another sixty official visitors were present. The conference opened on April 4 with an address by Dr. Henry Jessup, who had encouraged and given Sam sound advice when he first arrived in Beirut sixteen years before. Later in the day Sam presented a paper to the conference entitled *Statistical Surveys of the Mohammedan World*. As chairman of the Cairo Conference, Sam was also kept busy chairing meetings over the next several days. At these meetings, missionaries working in Muslim communities in Africa, India, Arabia, Southeast Asia, and even Bulgaria presented their prepared papers on a range of topics related to missionary work among Muslims.

By the time the conference came to a close on Monday, April 9, the delegates all agreed that their time together had been valuable, so much so that they voted to convene another meeting in five years in Lucknow, India.

At the end of the Cairo Conference, Sam headed back to the United States delighted and excited. He was delighted that all the organizing had come together to create a well-run and helpful conference, and he was excited about the impact the conference would have on future missionary work among Muslims.

Chapter 16

A Wider Ministry

Back with Amy and his family in the United States, Sam began writing another book, this one to be called *Islam, A Challenge to Faith*. The book would summarize all Sam had learned during the Cairo Conference. As he wrote, Sam was driven by the vision of hundreds of young Christians reading the book and setting out as missionaries to Muslims.

Although he longed to be back in Bahrain, Sam felt a pressing need to get out the message about Muslim evangelism and recruit more missionaries for the field. As it happened, he was presented with two opportunities to do just that. The first opportunity came when Dr. Fennel Turner, head of the Student Volunteer Movement in the United States, contacted Sam and offered him the position of traveling secretary. The position would entail his visiting college and university campuses and speaking at student conferences to educate, inspire, and recruit students to the mission field. The second opportunity came from the Reformed Church. The mission board wanted Sam to become Field Secretary for the Reformed Church Board of Foreign Missions.

Both offers were attractive to Sam. They both involved educating Christians about missions and would provide Sam ample opportunity to tell them about the needs of the Muslim world. Sam talked to Amy about the two offers and prayed earnestly about which one he should accept. Because he could not decide between the two, Sam, who was now forty years old, decided that he was still energetic enough to accept both positions. It would be hard work, he knew, but he was up for the challenge. An arrangement was worked out between the two organizations. The Reformed Church mission board agreed to continue paying Sam his missionary salary, and the Student Volunteer Movement would pay his traveling expenses.

In late 1907, the Zwemer moved from the Holland, Michigan, area to Mount Vernon, New York, to be near the headquarters of the two organizations Sam had agreed to work for. Shortly before they left, Amy gave birth to another daughter, whom they named Mary Moffatt Zwemer after the wife of David Livingstone, the famous missionary to Africa. Once they had settled into their new living quarters, Sam began his new job while Amy stayed home and tended to their four children—Bessie, age eight; Raymund, age five; Amy, age two; and newborn Mary.

The first places Sam visited as traveling secretary for the Student Volunteer Movement were Yale University, Auburn University, and the University of Virginia. Sam then began systematically visiting other universities and seminaries on the East Coast. When he was advertised as the speaker at various rallies and lectures, Sam placed the letters FRGS (Fellow of the Royal Geographic Society) after his name. After his lectures, many of those who came to hear him speak said they had done so because of his affiliation with the Royal Geographic Society. Sam smiled when he heard this and thought back to his visit to Sana'a, Yemen, sixteen years before. After that visit, on the boat back to Aden, several British officials had encouraged Sam to apply for membership to the Royal Geographic Society. Sam was glad he had followed their advice.

From colleges and seminaries on the East Coast, Sam went on to visit campuses in Oklahoma and Colorado. He also traveled to Europe to attend the Baslow Student Conference in England. And of course, he also kept busy as Field Secretary for the Reformed Church Board of Foreign Missions, speaking about missions in Reformed churches all over the country.

Whenever he traveled, whether by train or by ship, Sam used the time to write. He was pleased when *Islam, a Challenge to Faith* was published in 1907. He followed the book with two more: *The*

Unoccupied Mission Fields of Africa and Asia and *The Moslem Christ,* which traced the way Muslims and the Koran viewed Jesus. After these were published, he kept on writing.

On March 17, 1910, while still busily traveling the country and speaking at churches and on college campuses, Sam received word that his father had died at age eighty-seven. Sam and Amy and the children hurriedly made their way to Holland, Michigan, for his funeral, at which Sam spoke. As he stood in the Pilgrim's Home Cemetery in Graafschap and watched his father's coffin being lowered into the grave, Sam thought about his father's great influence. Adriaan had instilled in him—as he had in all his children—a deep-rooted Christian faith that sustained and guided all that Sam did. For that legacy Sam was grateful.

In May 1910, Sam's twin appointments with the Student Volunteer Movement and the Reformed Church Board of Foreign Missions came to an end. Sam thanked God for the opportunity he'd had to inspire thousands of young people to consider the call to missionary service. He was also thankful for those who had stepped forward to take up that call. One of them was William Borden at Yale University. William was a wealthy young man and heir to the Borden Dairy fortune. He declared his intention to Sam to work among the Muslims of China. Another was Paul Harrison, a medical student at Johns Hopkins University. Paul told Sam he wanted to serve on the most difficult mission field in the world. Once

Sam described to him the challenges of Arabia, Paul volunteered to serve with the Arabian Mission.

In the fall of 1910, the Zwemer family headed back to Bahrain. By now their daughter Bessie was eleven and Raymund was nine. After much prayer, Sam and Amy made the painful decision to leave their two oldest children behind with friends in Chicago so that they could complete their education in the United States. On September 10, 1910, Sam and Amy and their two young daughters, Amy Ruth and Mary, sailed from New York City aboard the liner *König Albert*. They had been away from Bahrain for five years.

After a long voyage, the Zwemers arrived in Bahrain on October 24. It felt good to be back. When Sam had left for furlough in 1905, sixteen missionaries had been serving with the Arabian Mission. Now the mission had twenty-nine missionaries, and in every mission station throughout Arabia the ministry was growing. Sam was amazed at how the ministry in Bahrain had developed in his absence. The hospital was still as busy as ever treating patients. Two new mission houses that accommodated eight missionaries had been constructed. In addition, there was a new two-story building with a chapel upstairs and a school for children downstairs. Boys and girls were taught in separate classes, where they learned Arabic, English, mathematics, geography, and science. Trees and gardens dotted the property, providing welcome shade in the heat of the day. To Sam it was like a Christian oasis in the midst of a physically and spiritually dry and barren land.

The Zwemer family quickly settled back into life in Bahrain, though Sam still spent a good deal of time traveling to speak at conferences. One of the conferences he traveled to in 1911 was the Lucknow Conference on Missions to Moslems, held at Lucknow in Northern India. This was the follow-up to the Cairo Conference held five years before, and once again Sam served as conference chairman. In Cairo, sixty-two delegates had been present at the conference, representing twenty-nine different mission societies. At the Lucknow Conference, 166 delegates were present, representing six different countries and fifty-eight different missionary societies. Sam was amazed by the growth of the conference. Once again, under his chairmanship the conference was a great success.

As Sam traveled from conference to conference to speak, he realized that his heart was no longer in the day-to-day work in Bahrain. He still loved the people of Bahrain and the mission work he had played such a big part in developing. But now he wanted to work in an interdenominational way, both informing the Christian church of the great need for Muslim evangelization and inspiring hundreds of Christians to join the worldwide missionary effort to Muslims. To this end Sam had started a magazine called *The Moslem World*. The first issue had been published in January 1911 to coincide with the Lucknow Conference. *The Moslem World* was a quarterly magazine designed to inform, inspire, and unite the Christian world to reach out to Muslims.

Sam wanted to reach out in an even broader way to the Christian church. The question was how to do so. The answer came in 1912 from several mission boards in Cairo, including the United Presbyterian Mission to Egypt, the Church Missionary Society, and the Nile Mission Press. Because of his successful leadership of the conferences in Cairo and Lucknow and his intellectual ability as demonstrated by the many books he had written on the Muslim world, Sam was now a recognized Christian leader in the field of understanding Islam. Since Cairo was considered the intellectual center of the Muslim world, at the crossroads of Africa and Arabia, these mission boards suggested that Sam move to Cairo and use it as a base for further study on Islam. The leaders of the mission societies felt that with Sam's presence in Cairo, the city would become a kind of intellectual center for Christians and missionary societies focused on missionary work among Muslims.

Sam was certainly fascinated by the proposal. He began to think of all the possibilities of living and working in such a hub of cultural activity as Cairo. Sam's only hesitation in moving ahead with such a plan was that it meant leaving behind the Arabian Mission he had helped found. As he pondered what to do, Sam wrote to the mission board of the Reformed Church in the United States. He was overjoyed when he received a response from them. The Reformed Church was willing to allow Sam to live in Cairo and work with many different denominations and Christian organizations as long as he made regular visits home to the United States to represent the Arabian Mission there. It was the just kind of response Sam had been praying for.

By October 1912, the Zwemer family had relocated from Bahrain to Cairo. On the day after Christmas that year, Sam wrote a newsletter to his family and supporters telling them how things were going.

> My three months' residence here in this great metropolis has already confirmed my judgment that it is the one strategic place in the Muslim world from which we can influence every Muslim land, persistently and irresistibly through the printed page. . . . Egypt has practically become a British protectorate. Both Mr. Upson and [I] have had personal interviews with Lord Kitchener [British consulgeneral in Egypt] and he is in full sympathy with the work. . . . Some of our special literature for Muslims has been translated during the year and printed in India, South Africa, Persia, and China.

Sam went on to explain in the newsletter that negotiations were under way to buy a new, bigger building for the Nile Mission Press and that he was busy writing a series of tracts for Muslim people. One tract was titled *Do You Pray?* It became so popular that people started addressing Sam as Mr. Do You Pray.

That Christmas the Zwemers also hosted William Borden, the heir to the Borden Dairy fortune, whom Sam had steered toward missions. William was in Cairo preparing to enter China and work among

Muslims. While still in Cairo, he became sick and was hospitalized. Sam and Amy visited him regularly at the hospital and prayed for him. William was diagnosed with cerebral meningitis. His condition grew worse until he died on April 9, 1913. A small group of missionaries stood at the gravesite to honor William's life. Sam conducted the funeral service and read a passage from *Pilgrim's Progress* about the death of Valiant Truth. News of the death of "Borden of Yale" reverberated around the Christian world. Construction of the Borden Memorial Hospital in memory of William Borden soon began in Lanchow, China.

In Cairo Sam produced his magazine *The Moslem World*, paying for most of its production out of his own pocket. He studied Islam and wrote books about it from a Christian perspective. He also worked closely with the Nile Mission Press to produce Christian literature for Muslims. Sam described printed pages as "leaves for the healing of the nations." He put his belief in the power of the printed page this way: "[The printed page] has a unique value as a means of carrying the gospel to Mohammedans . . . [it] finds an entrance into many doors closed to the living witness and can proclaim the gospel persistently, fearlessly and effectively."

Although the Zwemers were headquartered in Cairo, Sam spent much of his time traveling the world to speak at and attend conferences. On his travels, he researched Muslim groups and met with missionaries to find out what their needs were. He took Christian literature for Muslims (published by the Nile Mission Press) with him wherever he went.

In 1914, when the Great War broke out in Europe, little effect was felt in Egypt. The British kept a tight military rein on the country. Even when the Allies fought to wrestle control of Arabia away from the Turks, things remained stable in Egypt. Sam continued studying and writing. With the buildup of British and Allied troops in the country, Sam was in demand to preach to the troops, which he gladly did.

Even as the war raged in Europe, Sam made several visits there to speak. The war made travel more difficult, especially when he had to travel to the United States to attend a conference. Because of repeated German U-boat attacks on transatlantic passenger ships, Sam sailed to the United States by going in the opposite direction across the Pacific Ocean and landing on the West Coast in San Francisco. It was not the preferred route to get to the United States from Egypt, but he did arrive safely.

Whenever he was in the United States, Sam visited and spent time with Bessie and Raymund. Both children were doing well and receiving an excellent education. Sam was always sad to leave his oldest two children behind and travel on. When she could, Amy traveled with Sam to conferences and speaking engagements. Sam enjoyed her company as well as her wit and wisdom.

In 1924, Sam and Amy traveled overland from Cairo to Baghdad to speak at a large Christian conference. Traversing the blistering Arabian Desert was grueling, but it was something Sam and Amy seemed to relish. When they reached Baghdad, Jim was waiting to welcome them. Sam was excited to see his old friend, and the two men were able to spend time together praying, talking, and reminiscing about how the mission they had cofounded had grown and blossomed in Arabia.

From Baghdad Sam and Amy traveled to Basrah, the city where they had first met twenty-nine years before. Then it was off to Bahrain. This was the first time Sam had set foot on the island since he had left twelve years earlier, and he was impressed by what he saw. The mission had continued to grow, new buildings had been erected, the schools had grown, and there was now an Arabic printing press and a library along with a mission bookstore. Sam noticed one other curiosity on the Bahraini skyline—windmills. The first windmill on the island had been erected when Sam was overseeing the building of the hospital. It was designed to pump fresh water for use in the hospital. Back then, most of the residents of Bahrain had thought such a device crazy, but over the years, attitudes had changed. Now windmills had become the accepted way to pump fresh water from the ground.

During April and May of 1925, Sam visited England for twenty-three days. During that time he gave thirty-six addresses to over thirty-seven thousand people, earning himself the nickname the "Flying Dutchman."

After the trip to England, Sam and Amy traveled to the United States. The Zwemer family all met together in Alexandria, Virginia, to celebrate the marriage of Bessie Zwemer to the Reverend Claude

Pickens, a young Episcopal minister, on August 27, 1925. Sam and Amy were proud of their daughter, particularly her choice of a husband. Claude was a devout and energetic Christian with a desire to become a missionary.

Following Bessie and Claude's wedding, Sam and Amy headed back to Europe to speak in churches and at conferences in the Netherlands, Denmark, Sweden, Finland, Germany, and Italy before taking a steamer back to Egypt. In 1927 Sam went to the Balkans to learn more about the Muslims who lived there and investigate opportunities to proclaim the gospel.

By the beginning of 1929, Sam and Amy had spent seventeen years traveling the world, encouraging, learning, writing, speaking, and praying about missionary work among Muslims. Sam had a growing sense that things were about to change.

Chapter 17

Night Shall End in Day

In the fall of 1929, Sam sat down to write a letter to his friends in the Arabian Mission.

When the call came to leave Bahrain for the larger opportunities and wider tasks of the Nile Mission Press and the training of workers in Egypt, the pull at our heart strings was strong and we left Arabia with many regrets at parting from the circle of the mission. But as we look back over the seventeen years spent from Cairo as a base in travel and thought for the evangelization of the Muslim World, in the preparation of literature and its circulation, in helping forward in some small way the plans of other pioneer missions in Africa

and Southeastern Europe—we are convinced
that the call was of God. Once again—not suddenly, but by a series of Providences and calls
to service—we have moved our hearthstone
to a new center where we humbly trust that
God will use us for the same task, although in
another way.

In his letter Sam was referring to the position he
had accepted to become the chair of the History of
Religion and Christian Missions at Princeton University in Princeton, New Jersey. He and Amy had
prayed long and hard about the decision to leave the
Middle East and return to the United States as their
base of operation. In the end, Sam accepted the position because he wanted to be able to inspire some
of the brightest young minds in America to take up
the challenge of missionary work, especially among
Muslims.

In typical Zwemer style, Sam and Amy threw
themselves into their new roles at Princeton. The
Princeton Theological Seminary at the university was
part of the Presbyterian Church. It provided room
and board to twelve missionary families from all over
the world who were home on furlough. Sam took a
special interest in these missionaries, and Amy often
invited them over to their house for a home-cooked
meal and encouraging conversation. Always full of
ideas, Sam soon developed a weekly Round Table
Conference on missions. The weekly conference was
attended by the missionaries in residence and by students who were interested in missionary work.

Sam continued to write books and publish *The Moslem World* quarterly magazine. From the time he had started writing, Sam had managed to publish one book a year. Several of the books, those about the plight of Muslim women and children, were written in collaboration with Amy. Now that he had an office and a well-stocked library, Sam wrote even more. One of his most popular books during this period was *The Origin of Religion*, which he wrote as a textbook for a course he was teaching. The book soon became widely used in universities around the world.

Sam also accepted many speaking engagements that took him on tours around the world. He was in the British Isles in the summer of 1932 and in Northwest China the following year. Sam and Amy made time to visit their ever-growing family. By now all four of their children were married. Bessie and her husband, Claude, were missionaries in China. Raymund completed his medical degree and attended Yale and Harvard universities. Amy married a man named Homer Violette. Mary married Robert Brittain, a poet and author. Between them, their four children provided Sam and Amy with fifteen grandchildren.

The years teaching at Princeton flew by, and in May 1936 the family gathered to celebrate Sam and Amy's fortieth wedding anniversary. They were both still in excellent health and looked forward to spending a long and happy retirement together. Less than a year later, however, tragedy struck. Amy had gone to New York City to participate in the anniversary of the Women's Board of Foreign Missions. At the event she suffered a heart attack and was taken to the hospital. Sam received an urgent phone call to come to her side. But by the time he arrived in New York City, Amy had died.

Sam was stunned by the death of his wife. He broke down and wept as he thought of all the experiences they had shared. He remembered the first time he saw Amy—a pretty, young nurse—and how she had managed to pull the tablecloth and the best china off the table in Basrah; how he had helped her study Arabic in Baghdad and fallen in love with her quiet determination and intelligence; their wedding at the British consulate in Baghdad; the birth of six children and the death of Katharine and Ruth in Bahrain thirty-three years before; how Amy never complained about the constant traveling or the need to leave their children behind in the United States while they returned to the mission field. Unable to think how else to pay homage to his lifelong companion, Sam wrote a poem:

> Her love was like an island
> In life's ocean, vast and wide,
> A peaceful, quiet shelter
> From the wind and rain and tide.
> 'Twas bound on the north by Hope,
> By Patience on the west,
> By tender Counsel on the south
> And on the east by Rest.
> Above it, like a beacon light,
> Shone faith and truth and prayer;
> And through the changing scenes of life
> I found a haven there.

The Zwemer family gathered in Michigan to honor Amy's vibrant faith and Christian service. They buried her alongside the other members of the Zwemer family in Pilgrim's Home Cemetery in Graafschap. Now, at seventy years of age, Sam felt adrift and alone without Amy. Princeton University had a strict rule that faculty members must retire at age seventy. The school made an exception for Sam, allowing him one more year of teaching and giving him time to adjust to the sudden loss of his wife.

Soon after his official retirement from Princeton, Sam moved to Manhattan in New York City, where he rented rooms at the Carteret Hotel, just off Seventh Avenue on Twenty-Third Street. Even though he was officially retired, there seemed to be more than ever for him to do. Sam preached in churches and at conferences, prepared new books and tracts, and met with old friends.

In September 1939, just as war was breaking out in Europe, Sam had dinner with Jim, who was now also retired and whose his wife had died in 1927 after a long illness. Jim invited two women along for the evening to dine with him and Sam, and Sam found one of them, Miss Margaret Clarke, fascinating. Although Margaret was only fifty years old and Sam seventy-three, he invited her out to several events and the two of them fell in love. They were married on March 12, 1940, and moved into an apartment on Thirty-Third Street in Manhattan.

Sam was grateful to again have a wife at his side. Sometimes Margaret laughed that he had needed to marry a younger woman to keep up with him. Together Sam and Margaret made a formidable team. In one month they traveled by train across the United States twice, and Sam spoke at over forty-five events and services.

In 1947, Sam turned eighty years old, but he showed no signs of slowing down. Invitations to speak poured in, and Margaret began making plans for them to travel to Kuwait to celebrate the sixtieth anniversary of the Arabian Mission in 1949.

When they arrived, it felt strange for Sam to be standing in Basrah and reminiscing. He wished Jim could have been there with him, but Jim had died in 1940, soon after Sam and Margaret were married. How the city had changed! Sam could hardly recognize it as the same place where he and Jim had opened the first station for the Arabian Mission.

From Basrah Sam traveled on to Bahrain. What a transformation awaited him there! Oil derricks now dominated the skyline, and everywhere he looked, air conditioners poked from the windows of houses. The Mason Memorial Hospital was now a huge, sprawling facility, but it still carried on the same mission: to show God's love to people through acts of compassion and care.

While he was in Bahrain, Sam visited the cemetery where Katharine and Ruth were buried. Their grave was overgrown with weeds, which Sam cleared away before saying a prayer over it. Sam knew all too well that total commitment to serving God and proclaiming the gospel often came at a high cost.

From Bahrain Sam traveled to Kuwait, where he spoke at the sixtieth anniversary celebration of the Arabian Mission and was the guest of honor.

As he reflected on this visit to Arabia, Sam wrote, "Challenged by the opportunity for evangelism among both Arab- and English-speaking communities, the mission called for large reinforcement and for prevailing prayer. The burden of Arabia is Islam, but that burden is being lifted. God's providence and His gospel are at work."

Soon after Sam and Margaret returned to New York from Arabia, Margaret became sick. She was hospitalized, and her condition declined. She died on February 21, 1950, at the age of sixty.

Sam accompanied the body of his second wife to Michigan for burial in the family plot in Pilgrim's Home Cemetery in Graafschap. He had expected Margaret to outlive him, and he found it hard to believe she was really gone. But still he carried on. He wrote an article about his favorite hymn, "Christian, Dost Thou See Them?" The words of the hymn were written by St. Andrew of Crete around the year 700. Sam found particular comfort in the last verse:

Christian, dost thou hear them
How they speak thee fair?
Always fast and vigil? Always watch and prayer?
Christian, answer boldly:
"While I breathe I pray."
Peace shall follow battle,
Night shall end in day.

By now Sam knew he was nearing the end of his own life, and he took as his motto the line from the hymn, "While I breathe I pray."

A year later Sam attended the General Synod of the Reformed Church in Pennsylvania. During the event he began to feel ill. A doctor told him that he had a serious heart condition and there was nothing that could be done about it. Sam decided to soldier on until the end. He preached in New York City, and in Virginia in February 1952 he addressed the missionary conference of the InterVarsity Christian Fellowship. The night after the address he was hospitalized, and in March he was transferred to a convalescent home, where he preached at the Sunday services to the other patients.

On Wednesday, April 2, 1952, Samuel Marinus Zwemer died quietly, ten days short of his eightyfifth birthday.

After a stirring funeral service held at the First Presbyterian Church of New York City, many people read the words that Sam had penned four years before, intended for a conference in England he was unable to attend.

How memory brings back the occasions when we met together, and the happy hours spent in prayer and Christian fellowship. I am now in my 81st year and have spent sixty years thinking of the Moslem World and its problems! It began when I signed a card in 1886 expressing the purpose to become a foreign missionary! Little did I realize all the ways God would lead me into Arabia and Egypt and across the world of Islam, and guide my pen to call to others.

"With mercy and with judgment
My web of time He wove
And aye the dews of sorrow
Were lustered by His love."

Never have I regretted choosing a hard field and an impossible task. How much has changed for the better, and how many doors have opened in Arabia since 1890, and in all Asia and Africa. God's providence has been so visible that all may see His purpose. We must not lose faith or courage, but be earnest and steadfast and diligent until the going down of our sun—or the rising of His Son at His glorious appearing.

Sam's children escorted his body back to Michigan, where Sam was laid to rest in the family plot in Pilgrim's Home Cemetery in Graafschap. His family sang from his favorite hymn, "Peace shall follow battle, night shall end in day."

Arabian Mission Newsletters, 1892–1962. The Arabian Mission.

Jessup, Henry Harris. *Kamil Abdul Messiah: The Setting of the Crescent and the Rising of the Cross.* Philadelphia: Westminster Press, 1898.

Mason, Alfred DeWitt, and Frederick Jacob Barny. *History of the Arabian Mission.* New York: Board of Foreign Missions Reformed Church in America, 1926.

Report of the Fourth Decennial Indian Missionary Conference held in Madras: December 11–18, 1902. Christian Literature Society, 1902.

Scudder, Lewis R. III. *The Arabian Mission's Story: In Search of Abraham's Other Son.* Grand Rapids: Wm. B. Eerdmans, 1998.

Wilson, J. Christy. *Apostle to Islam: A Biography of Samuel M. Zwemer.* Grand Rapids: Baker Book House, 1952.

Zwemer, Adrian. *Genealogy and History of the Zwemer-Boon Family: Recorded for His Children.* Harrisburg, PA: Nungesser, 1932.

Zwemer, Samuel Marinus, and James Cantine. *The Golden Milestone: Reminiscences of Pioneer Days Fifty Years Ago in Arabia.* New York: Fleming H. Revell, 1938

Janet and Geoff Benge are a husband and wife writing team with more than twenty years of writing experience. Janet is a former elementary school teacher. Geoff holds a degree in history. Originally from New Zealand, the Benges spent ten years serving with Youth With A Mission. They have two daughters, Laura and Shannon, and an adopted son, Lito. They make their home in the Orlando, Florida, area.

Also from Janet and Geoff Benge...
Christian Heroes: Then & Now

More adventure-filled biographies for ages 10 to 100!

Elisabeth Elliot: Joyful Surrender • *978-1-57658-513-9*
Paul Brand: Helping Hands • *978-1-57658-536-8*
D. L. Moody: Bringing Souls to Christ • *978-1-57658-552-8*
Dietrich Bonhoeffer: In the Midst of Wickedness • *978-1-57658-713-3*
Francis Asbury: Circuit Rider • *978-1-57658-737-9*
Samuel Zwemer: The Burden of Arabia • *978-1-57658-738-6*

Unit Study Curriculum Guides
Turn a great reading experience into an even greater
learning opportunity with a Unit Study Curriculum Guide.
Available for select biographies.

Available from YWAM Publishing
1-800-922-2143 / www.ywampublishing.com